THE ROUGH GUIDE TO THE
USA's
NATIONAL
PARKS

THE ROUGH GUIDE TO THE
USA's
NATIONAL
PARKS

DISTRIBUTION

UK, Ireland and Europe
Apa Publications (UK) Ltd; sales@roughguides.com

United States and Canada
Ingram Publisher Services; ips@ingramcontent.com

Australia and New Zealand
Booktopia; retailer@booktopia.com.au

Worldwide
Apa Publications (UK) Ltd; sales@roughguides.com

SPECIAL SALES, CONTENT LICENSING
AND CO-PUBLISHING

Rough Guides can be purchased in bulk quantities at discounted prices. We can create special editions, personalized jackets and corporate imprints tailored to your needs. sales@roughguides.com.
roughguides.com

Printed in China

HELP US UPDATE

We've gone to a lot of effort to ensure that this first edition of The Rough Guide to the USA's National Parks is accurate and up-to-date. But if you feel we've got it wrong or left something out, we'd like to know.
Please send your comments with the subject line "Rough Guides USA's National Parks Update" to mail@uk.roughguides.com. We'll credit all contributions and send a copy of the next edition (or any other Rough Guide if you prefer) for the very best emails.

THE ROUGH GUIDE TO THE
USA'S NATIONAL PARKS

Editors: Sarah Clark and Aimee White
Picture editors: Piotr Kala and Tom Smyth
Designer: Michal Ptasznik
Typesetter: Daniel May
Head of DTP and Pre-Press: Rebeka Davies
Head of Publishing: Sarah Clark

THE ROUGH GUIDE TO THE
USA's NATIONAL PARKS

INTRODUCTION

The towering snow-capped peaks of the Northern Cascades and Rocky Mountains; the shimmering Gateway Arch, soaring over St Louis; the vast, water-logged sawgrass plains of Florida's Everglades; the immense icefields and glaciers of Alaska; and the steaming volcanoes of Hawaii.

These are just some of the incredibly diverse National Parks of the United States. In one country, you can stroll through the giant redwoods of California, soak up the mesmerizing vistas in Crater Lake and Yosemite, stand in awe at the Grand Canyon, delve into a subterranean wonderland at Mammoth Cave, and cruise Lake Superior to forest-bound Isle Royale. Ever since the creation of Yellowstone in 1872, national parks have protected a portion of precious American wilderness from the ravages of "progress", to leave room for the bears and butterflies, wildflowers and ancient forests.

But the parks are more than islands of nature. They are sanctuaries of the human heart. To Native Americans, these landscapes are still sacred ground. Landmarks like the Black Hills and the Grand Canyon are part of a spiritual topography. Different tribes can point to mountains, forests, rivers and canyons and declare, "This is where our people came from". They can point to the ruins of ancient villages and say, "These are the footprints of our ancestors".

More than just pretty places where one can snap a few pictures, the national parks are an acknowledgment of the human need for wilderness. These are places where there's room for lone hikers to lose, or find, themselves; for mountaineers to test their mettle against the elements; for scientists to study the natural world in a nearly pristine environment; for ordinary visitors to gape at something greater than themselves and let their dreams run wild.

ESSENTIAL INFORMATION

Founded in 1916, the US National Park Service is an agency of the US Department of the Interior, with its head office in Washington, D.C. (1849 C Street NW). For general information about the parks, visit www.nps.gov. For campground and some tour reservations, visit Recreation.gov (many campgrounds are first come, first served, however).

Opening hours: Hours at park facilities vary from site to site and season to season. During peak months, park facilities tend to stay open 8.30am–6pm, seven days a week; some desert park visitor centers may open earlier in the summer to allow visitors to make a start during the cooler time of day.

Hours may be limited during the off-season, and some mountain parks suspend facilities completely during winter. Holiday closings, if any, may include Thanksgiving, Christmas, and New Year's Day.

Information is also available from the following regional offices:

Alaska Regional Office, 240 West 5th Ave, Anchorage, AK 99501, tel: 907-644-3470; nps.gov/orgs/1840/index.htm

Intermountain Region, 12795 West Alameda Parkway, Lakewood, CO 80228, tel: 303-987-6690; nps.gov/orgs/1072/index.htm

Midwest Regional Office, 601 Riverfront Drive, Omaha, NE 68102, tel: 402-661-1904; nps.gov/orgs/1671/index.htm

National Trails System, Conservation and Outdoor Recreation, 1849 C Street NW, Washington, D.C. 20240, tel: 202-354-6900; nps.gov/subjects/nationaltrailssystem/index.htm

National Capital Regional Office, 1100 Ohio Drive SW, Washington, D.C. 20242, tel: 202-619-7180; nps.gov/orgs/1465/index.htm

Northeast Regional Office, 1234 Market St, Philadelphia, PA 19107, tel: 215-597-1578; nps.gov/orgs/1651/index.htm

Pacific West Region, 333 Bush St, Suite 500, San Francisco, CA 94104-2828, tel: 415-623-2100; nps.gov/orgs/1180/index.htm

Southeast Region Atlanta Federal Center, 1924 Building, 100 Alabama St SW, Atlanta, GA 30303, tel: 404-507-5792.

Other federal public lands are administered by:

Bureau of Land Management, US Department of the Interior, 1849 C Street NW, Rm. 5665, Washington DC 20240, tel: 202-208-3801; www.blm.gov.

US Fish and Wildlife Service, US Department of the Interior, 1849 C Street NW, Washington, D.C. 20240, tel: 800 344 9453; www.fws.gov.

US Forest Service, 1400 Independence Ave SW, Washington, D.C. 20250, tel: 800-832-1355; www.fs.fed.us.

Denali peak

DENALI

Dominated by the mighty peak of its namesake mountain, Denali National Park lies at the heart of the Alaska Range, a land of snow-capped summits and blissfully untrammelled wilderness. Thrusting mightily against the sky at a height of 20,310ft, Denali itself is North America's tallest peak – its Athabaskan name means 'The Great One'. Denali's great height, combined with its subarctic location, makes it one of the coldest mountains on the planet. Climbing it is extremely demanding and requires some proficiency in basic mountaineering skills; the climb begins on the Kahiltna Glacier and takes an exhausting 17–18 days round trip from Base Camp.

But the great peak's magnetism also tugs on those who'll never climb its slopes. Nearly everyone who travels into the park sees at least one of Alaska's 'big four': grizzly bear, Dall sheep, moose or caribou. Wolves have also become increasingly visible in recent years. It's not by chance that Denali offers such wildlife riches. Situated 240 miles northwest of Anchorage, the park was established in 1917 to protect the region's large mammals, especially Dall sheep, from hunting. The park is also perfect for short hiking forays into the wilderness. Trails run off from Denali Park Road, which runs west from the main entrance, through boggy tundra, more than 92 miles (148km) to Kantishna.

Wolf walking in the snow

Caribou crossing road sign

Talkeetna

Dall sheep in the Alaska Range

Grizzly bear

Glacier hiking

Bull moose in Wonder Lake

Denali Visitor Centre welcome sign

From the Denali Visitor Center, the two-mile (3.2km) long Savage River Loop is a mellow tramp along the gurgling, braided river, studded with gravel bars. Primrose Ridge (Mile 16) is an open, high alpine area where Dall Sheep often graze, and wildflowers bloom in spring and early summer. In autumn, the area is ablaze with red-leafed dwarf birch trees and orange tundra.

From the Eielson Visitor Center at Mile 66, located near the base of Denali, the Thorofare Ridge Trail is a very steep hike of around 1000ft – the top offers magnificent views of Denali, with mountains rolling out of the horizon like fangs. Located at Mile 85, the limpid waters of tranquil Wonder Lake beautifully reflect the snowy summits around it. Beavers can often be seen at the Wonder Lake Inflow, usually early in the morning or later at night. The McKinley River Bar Trail leads from the lake campground to the wide McKinley River through spruce forest and past several small ponds. It's especially spectacular in June, when wildflowers pepper the tundra with colour, or early autumn, when wild blueberries litter the trail.

Driving through Denali Park

Village marker for Wiseman Alaska

Wolverine

Black bear

Dalton Highway

GATES OF THE ARCTIC

Four times larger than Yellowstone, the Gates of the Arctic National Park girdles the central Brooks Range, the Rocky Mountains' northernmost extension. The 13,200-sq-mile unit lies entirely above the Arctic Circle and has some of the continent's wildest, most fragile ecosystems. Its forests, alder thickets and tundra are home to numerous mammal species , including grizzly and black bears, wolves, moose, Dall sheep, caribou and wolverines. The park is named after its two primary attractions: peaks known as Boreal Mountain and Frigid Crags, that loom astride the North Fork of the Koyukuk River, appearing to pioneers as the literal "Gates of the Arctic".

Most of the park is untamed wilderness. Capping the Brooks Range are wave upon wave of mountain ridges and jagged peaks – most of them nameless – that seem to stretch forever. The mountains are dissected by expansive U-shaped valleys that magnify the sense of wide-open spaces. Among the streams knifing through the park are six officially designated 'wild rivers.' Chief visitor attractions, besides the Gates, include 8510ft-Mount Igikpak, serene Walker Lake and a group of towering granite spires called the Arrigetch Peaks. 'Arrigetch' means 'fingers of the hand extended' in the language of the Nunamuit Iñupiat; their legends say that the Creator placed his glove on the land here as a reminder of his presence.

McBride Glacier in the eastern arm of the park

Exploring the one of the many inlets by kayak

Forest Loop Trail

GLACIER BAY

Accessible only by boat or seaplane, Glacier Bay National Park remains a spectacular, icy wilderness, largely untouched by modern development. 62 miles (100km) long and surrounded by a horseshoe rim of mountains, the bay is best known for its 17 tidewater glaciers, though Grand Pacific Glacier, which carved the bay, has receded over 20 miles (32km) since the 1800s. In

summer, orcas, minkes, and humpbacks frolic in the bay, while porpoises, sea otters, sea lions, harbour seals, and seabirds frequent its waters year round, and bears, wolves, moose, and mountain goats prowl its shores. The landscape also shows the stages of plant succession left by a retreating glacier: lush coastal forests give way to fields of willow and alder, soft shrubby mats, and, finally, barren grey rock and blue ice. The bay has about a dozen inlets or arms to explore – one reason it's considered a kayakers' paradise.

Beyond Glacier Bay itself, the park encompasses miles and miles of rugged, rarely visited coastline. Inland are huge ice fields, dozens of glaciers, legions of unnamed and unclimbed mountains, and a portion of the spectacular Alsek River, born in neighbouring British Columbia.

KATMAI

For most of its existence, Katmai National Park's primary appeals have been sportfishing for rainbow trout and salmon, and the Valley of 10,000 Smokes, formed in 1912 by a giant volcanic eruption. The eruption caused the collapse of Mount Katmai, devastated the surrounding landscape and created thousands of steaming fumaroles (only a few active vents remain). There are still at least 14 active volcanoes in Katmai, more than in any other national park.

Today, however, the fly-in only park is best known for its easy-to-see brown bears. In early July, thousands of bright, silvery sockeye salmon push upstream toward Brooks Lake. As they near their spawning grounds, the salmon face one final obstacle: 5ft-high Brooks Falls. Following the salmon to Brooks Falls is the brown bear. Coastal equivalents of grizzlies, up to a dozen bears may gather at the falls in July, with 35–40 bears inhabiting the 1.5-mile (2.5km)-long Brooks River drainage (there are over 2000 bears in the entire park). Visitors can observe the bears snatching fish mid-air with jaws or paws from the Brooks Falls viewing platform. Open since the 1940s, seasonal Brooks Camp acts as a service centre for the area. Beyond Brooks lies a vast untrammelled wilderness that includes the barren, lava-strewn Valley of 10,000 Smokes, glacier-covered mountains, the Alagnak Wild River, and a rugged fjord-like coast.

Grizzly bear in Kinak Bay

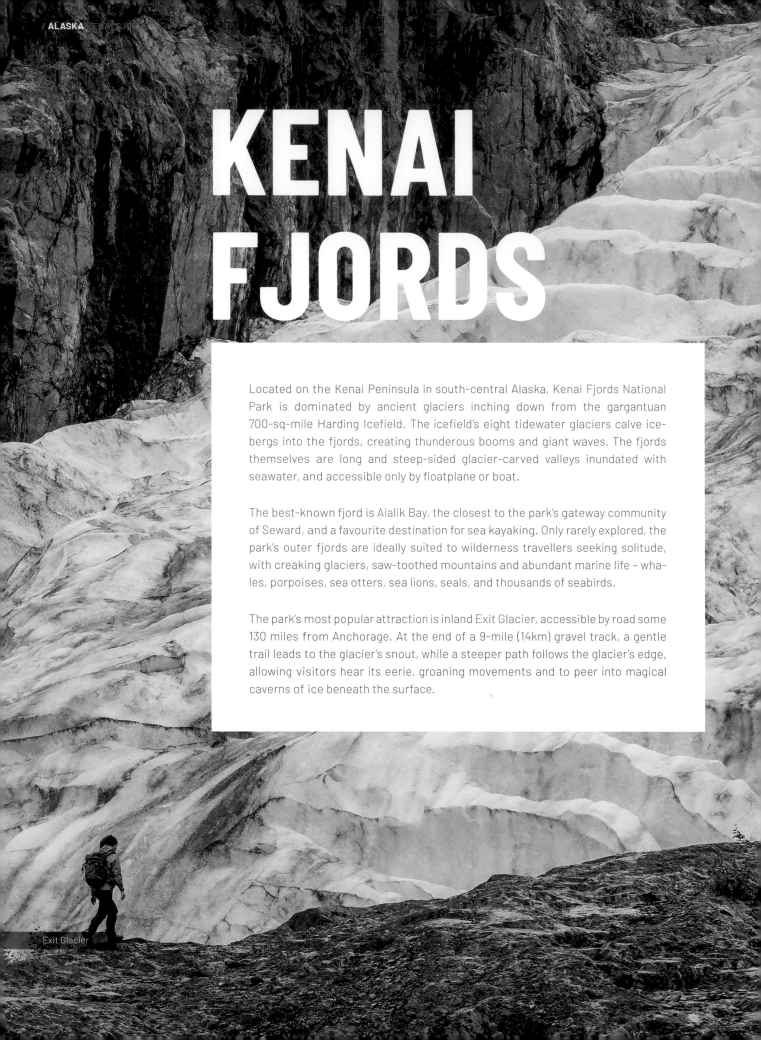

KENAI FJORDS

Located on the Kenai Peninsula in south-central Alaska, Kenai Fjords National Park is dominated by ancient glaciers inching down from the gargantuan 700-sq-mile Harding Icefield. The icefield's eight tidewater glaciers calve icebergs into the fjords, creating thunderous booms and giant waves. The fjords themselves are long and steep-sided glacier-carved valleys inundated with seawater, and accessible only by floatplane or boat.

The best-known fjord is Aialik Bay, the closest to the park's gateway community of Seward, and a favourite destination for sea kayaking. Only rarely explored, the park's outer fjords are ideally suited to wilderness travellers seeking solitude, with creaking glaciers, saw-toothed mountains and abundant marine life – whales, porpoises, sea otters, sea lions, seals, and thousands of seabirds.

The park's most popular attraction is inland Exit Glacier, accessible by road some 130 miles from Anchorage. At the end of a 9-mile (14km) gravel track, a gentle trail leads to the glacier's snout, while a steeper path follows the glacier's edge, allowing visitors hear its eerie, groaning movements and to peer into magical caverns of ice beneath the surface.

Exit Glacier

Aialik glacier

Sea lions

Humpback whale

Lone caribou

Kobuk River

Rainbow over Kotzebue

KOBUK VALLEY

Deep in northwestern Alaska lies one of the strangest sights anywhere in America: 100ft-high sand dunes, north of the Arctic Circle. The Great Kobuk Sand Dunes are the centrepiece of Kobuk Valley National Park, rising from the spruce forests like glittering mounds of gold. This is one of Alaska's most remote preserves, with no designated trails or roads, and only accessible by boat or plane. Most visitors begin their trips in Kotzebue, an Iñupiat village 75 miles to the west.

Summer temperatures may exceed 90°F (32°C) in the ever-shifting dunes, made of ancient glacial sand carried to the Kobuk Valley by wind and the Kobuk River. Also within the park are two smaller sets of dunes, the Little Kobuk and Hunt River.

The Kobuk Valley is also an important autumn and winter range for the Western Arctic caribou herd; they can be seen crossing the Kobuk River from late August through October, during their annual migration. Caribou are an important food source for the region's Iñupiat residents, who have lived along the Kobuk for at least 12,000 years. Iñupiat still hunt caribou at a well-known archeological site called Onion Portage at the east end of the park.

Grizzly footprints

American Bald Eagle

Grizzly bear and two cubs

Mount Redoubt from Anchor Point

LAKE CLARK

Located on the western side of Cook Inlet in southwest Alaska, Lake Clark National Park epitomizes the wild, untamed north. Within its boundaries lie two active volcanoes: Mount Redoubt (which erupted in 2009) and Mount Iliamna, as well as its namesake Lake Clark and waterways crucial to the Bristol Bay salmon fishery. Watching brown bears fishing for spawning sockeye in the Kijik River and at Silver Salmon Creek is a popular activity here.

Only accessible by seaplane or boat, the park features a rugged coastline of soaring cliffs that serve as rookeries for multitudes of seabirds, as well as an untouched interior dominated by the snow-capped Chigmit and Neacola mountains. Crystal-clear Lake Clark itself is about 40 miles long and about 5 miles wide, backed by a wall of snowy peaks and ringed by dense spruce forests. Lakeside Port Alsworth serves as park headquarters and visitor centre. The park embraces a remarkably diverse mix of plant communities, from coastal rainforest to boreal forest, salt marsh and several varieties of tundra. The park's various ecosystems support at least 187 species of birds, including several pairs of bald and golden eagles and peregrine falcons, plus many mammal species, from tiny shrews to moose, Dall sheep and caribou.

Salmon catch in Lake Clark

Mount Wragnell

WRANGELL-ST ELIAS

A wild and magnificent alpine world, Wrangell-St. Elias National Park is - at 20,625 square miles - bigger than Switzerland and by far the nation's largest park. Within its boundaries lie four major mountain ranges and six of the continent's 10 highest peaks, including 18,008ft Mount St. Elias, as well as the Wrangell Volcanic Field. Made up of thousands of lava flows and towering craters, the latter includes Mount Wrangell, one of the largest (by volume) active volcanoes in the world and the only one active in the Wrangell Mountains - steam plumes often rise from its summit.

Here, too, is North America's largest subpolar icefield, the Bagley, which feeds a system of gigantic glaciers, including the Tana, Miles and Guyot. Rock walls rise thousands of feet above glacially carved canyons, like the Chitistone and Nizina. Rugged, remote coastline is bounded by tidewater glaciers and jagged peaks. One of the park's best-known overland routes, the primitive and rugged Goat Trail, was traditionally used by Athabaskan people for hunting and trading. Even today, Wrangell-St. Elias contains one of the largest concentrations of Dall sheep in North America. Moose are often seen near willow bogs and lakes, while in the autumn, bears may be sighted near salmon spawning streams. Other species of large mammals here include black bears, mountain goats, caribou and even two herds of transplanted bison.

Aircraft in McCarthy airport

Mountain goats

Kitted-out hiker

Sunset over the Grand Canyon's South Rim

Hiking along the South Rim

Desert Big Horn Ram

GRAND CANYON

No photograph, no statistics, can prepare you for the immensity of Grand Canyon National Park. At more than one mile deep, it's an inconceivable abyss; varying in its central stretch from four to eighteen miles wide, it's an endless expanse of bewildering shapes and colours, glaring desert brightness and impenetrable shadow, stark promontories and soaring, never-to-be-climbed sandstone pinnacles. Billions of years of the earth's geologic history is frozen in bright bands of pink, beige, orange, rust and gold on the canyon walls. Far below glides the Colorado River, which carved out the canyon some six billion years ago.

The main canyon access point is the South Rim, where the Rim Trail links a series of mesmerizing viewpoints, the panoramas from which shift and change unceasingly from dawn to dusk. The far-more isolated North Rim is quieter, but at one thousand feet higher this entire area is usually closed by snow from November until mid-May. Helicopter rides offer a birds-eye perspective of the canyon, while rafting trips traverse the river rapids far below. From either rim trails also snake down the canyon walls: you can hike or ride a mule along the Bright Angel, North and South Kaibab trails all the way down to the river.

Sunrise at Toroweap

A trek from the North Rim down the Kaibab Trail begins among cool aspen, spruce and fir. This forest is home to mule deer, coyote, mountain lion, wild turkey and the unusual white-tailed Kaibab squirrel. As the trail descends, conditions become steadily warmer and the forest cedes to species like pinyon, juniper and mountain mahogany. At about 5000ft, trees vanish altogether, giving way to a scrubland of blackbrush, yucca, Mormon tea and various cacti – the canyon floor is covered in the barrel cacti, ocotillo and mesquite trees associated with southern Arizona. Temperatures at the canyon bottom can reach 120°F. Water bursts from springs, seeps out of gravel in canyon bottoms and supports lush oases of vegetation, including willows and big, shady cottonwood trees. The streams are home to beavers, dippers, herons, rainbow trout, frogs and other undesert-like creatures. To really soak up the tranquillity of this otherworldly setting, it's possible to camp or spend the night at the rustic Phantom Ranch, built from local stone and wood in 1922, before making the demanding climb back to the top.

Pink cactus blooming

South Kaibab Trail

Black Bridge over the Colorado River

Springtime flora

Blue Mesa

Fallen red logs along Long Logs Walk

PETRIFIED FOREST

It's the sheer abundance of fossilized wood that makes Petrified Forest National Park so enchanting. Each year, ongoing erosion exposes more and more lithified logs, lying in haphazard profusion on the barren slopes. The wood-bearing layer, also rich in dinosaur bones and other fossils, extends 300ft beneath the ground. These gigantic trees date back 225 million years. In late afternoon, the setting sun brings out their rich red and orange hues.

Rough concrete walkways have been laid over the terrain – and often over the tree trunks too – so visitors can ramble through the larger concentrations of logs. At Blue Mesa, certain tree trunks are raised on muddy "pedestals" above the surrounding desert; at Agate Bridge, one even spans a little gully. On the Long Logs Walk, at the edge of the desert, a little grass manages to survive, making the half-mile main trail especially surreal. The large, shattered logs are simply strewn across the grasslands, with not another stone or rock in sight. A side trail leads in another half-mile to a knoll holding the remains of a 700-year-old pueblo constructed entirely from petrified wood.

The park also includes picturesque stretches of the Painted Desert, an area of multicoloured badlands that covers much of northeast Arizona. At different times of day, the undulating expanse of clay-topped mounds takes on different colours, with an emphasis on blueish shades of grey and reddish shades of brown.

Painted Desert

Orange cactus blossoming

Gila woodpecker

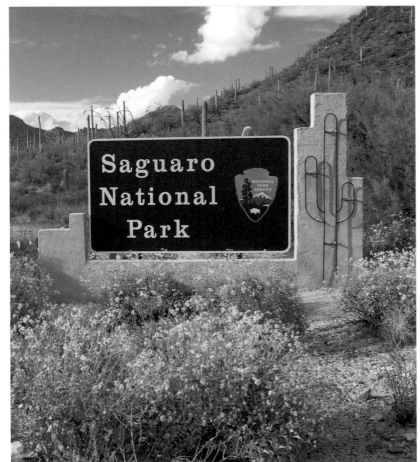

Saguaro National Park welcome sign

Tall cactus in Saguaro National Park

SAGUARO

Encompassing stretches of the arid Sonoran Desert in southeastern Arizona, Saguaro National Park offers visitors a rare and enthralling opportunity to stroll through desert "forests" of monumental, multi-limbed saguaro cactuses. These can grow up to 50ft tall, but they only reach full height after around 150 years. Each year, between late April and June, saguaros can grow up to a hundred white flowers, each of which blossoms for a single night. Woodpeckers and owls burrow holes into the trunk for their nests, while the Tohono O'odham people mashed the saguaro's succulent crimson fruit to make jam, syrup and even wine, and used its long, wood-like ribs to construct dwellings and fences.

The Tucson Mountain District of the park is traversed by the Bajada Loop Drive, which wriggles through a wonderland of twisted saguaro, offering plentiful short hiking trails and photo opportunities. The easiest walk, the Desert Discovery Nature Trail, follows a small gully before climbing onto a low brow for sweeping westward views, with abundant cacti all around. Further along the road lies Signal Hill, known for its magnificent sunset panoramas. The eastern section of the park, the Rincon Mountain District, is accessed by the Cactus Forest Drive loop. From the road, the Freeman Homestead Trail drops down to the barely visible vestiges of a pioneer home, then follows the course of a gentle wash back up again, threading between abundant groups of towering saguaro.

HOT SPRINGS

Much of the low-key, historic spa town of Hot Springs is preserved within this national park, nestled in the forested Zig Zag Mountains of central Arkansas. Early settlers fashioned a crude resort out of the wilderness here, and after the railroads arrived in 1875, it became a European-style spa; its thermal waters are said to cure rheumatism, arthritis, kidney disease and liver problems. Hot Springs is also a magnet for small art galleries, plenty of which line Central Avenue.

At the heart of the park is Bathhouse Row, eight magnificent buildings – built between 1912 and 1923 – behind a lush display of magnolia trees and elms. The grandest was the 1915 Fordyce Bathhouse, which now operates as the visitor centre for the National Park. The interiors are adorned with veined Italian marble, mosaic-tile floors and stained glass. The only establishment still open for business is the Buckstaff Bathhouse, in continuous operation since 1912. The nearby Ozark Bathhouse was built in 1922, designed in the Spanish Colonial Revival style, and now serves as a cultural centre. The park's forested areas – North Mountain and West Mountain – are laced with 26 miles of trails. The Sunset Trail is the longest, cutting through the most remote areas of the park. Trails also lead up the steep slopes of Hot Springs Mountain, through dense woods of oak, hickory and short-leafed pine.

Hot Springs, Zig Zag Mountains

CHANNEL ISLANDS

Lying off the coast of southern California, Channel Islands National Park preserves a chain of pristine desert islands, five accessible by boat or plane. Arid and barren for much of the year, winter rains transform Anacapa Island, when tree sunflowers smother the hills with bright yellow blossoms, along with fiery red Indian paintbrush, morning glory and pale buckwheat. The island's rugged cliffs are home to a huge colony of California brown pelicans, and the largest breeding colony of western gulls in the world. On the shore, the barks of sea lions and harbour seals echo across the water, while beneath the surface lie giant kelp forests.

West of Anacapa, Santa Cruz Island is also rich in fauna – including bald eagles, rare scrub jays and native foxes – and boasts diverse landscapes that range from forbidding canyons to tranquil green valleys, laced with spectacular hiking trails.

Santa Rosa Island features flatter terrain, with groves of rare Torrey pine. Home to the Chumash people until 1820, the island's archeological sites – some of which date back 13,000 years – are especially intriguing. Some fifty miles offshore, windswept San Miguel Island is alive with elephant seals and sea lions, while between late January and March remote Santa Barbara Island is carpeted in brilliant yellow tickseed flowers, poppies and verbena. Trails meander over low hills to overlooks with sensational coastal views.

Inspiration Point, Anacapa Island

Rocky arch off Anacapa Island

Lighthouse on Anacapa Island

Western Gull

Zabriskie Point

Extreme heat warning sign

Dry desert floor

Mesquite Flat Sand Dunes

Prickly Pear cactus

DEATH VALLEY

One of the hottest places on earth, dazzling Death Valley National Park is a land of rugged mountains, candy-coloured rocks and blistering deserts. Grand vistas sweep down from the subalpine slopes of Telescope Peak (11,000ft) to Badwater, a pool loaded with chloride and sulphates near the lowest point in the western hemisphere at 282ft below sea level; sharply silhouetted hills are eroded into deeply shadowed crevices, their exotic mineral content turning million-year-old mud flats into rainbows of sunlit phosphorescence; and stark hills harbour the bleached ruins of mining enterprises that briefly flourished against all odds. Sunrise and sunset are the best times to witness the vibrant colours that are usually bleached out by the midday sun, and they're also the most likely times for spotting wildlife. Despite its harsh environment, the park it is home to a great variety of creatures, from snakes and giant eagles to tiny fish and bighorn sheep.

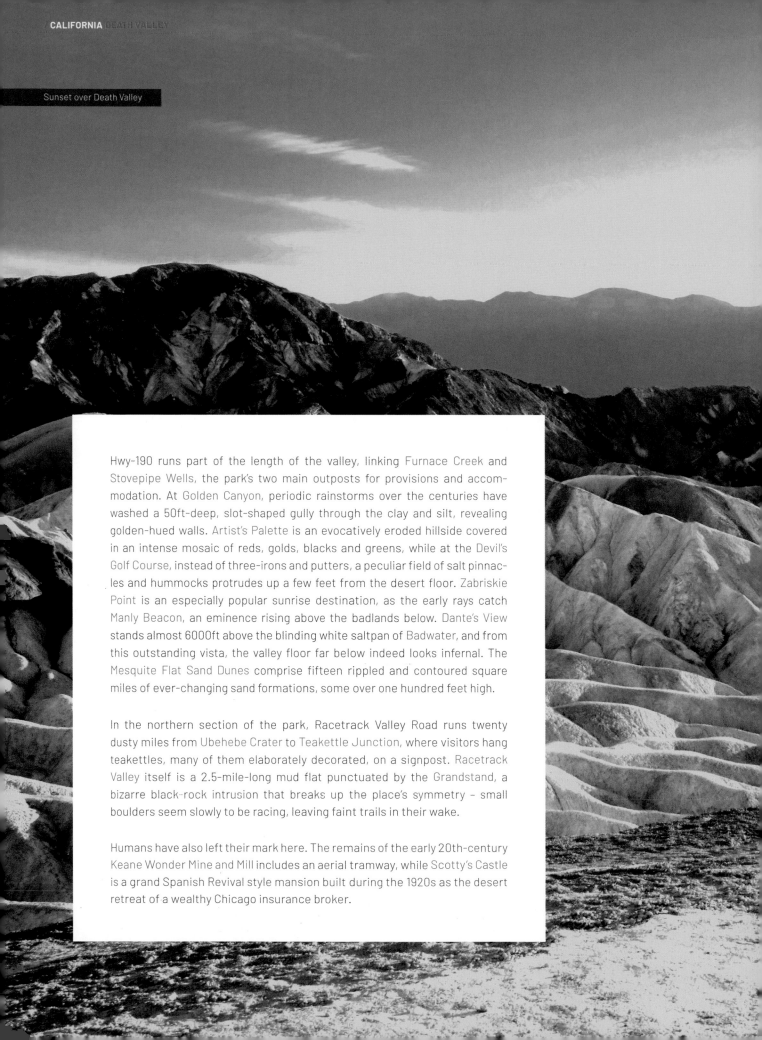

Sunset over Death Valley

Hwy-190 runs part of the length of the valley, linking Furnace Creek and Stovepipe Wells, the park's two main outposts for provisions and accommodation. At Golden Canyon, periodic rainstorms over the centuries have washed a 50ft-deep, slot-shaped gully through the clay and silt, revealing golden-hued walls. Artist's Palette is an evocatively eroded hillside covered in an intense mosaic of reds, golds, blacks and greens, while at the Devil's Golf Course, instead of three-irons and putters, a peculiar field of salt pinnacles and hummocks protrudes up a few feet from the desert floor. Zabriskie Point is an especially popular sunrise destination, as the early rays catch Manly Beacon, an eminence rising above the badlands below. Dante's View stands almost 6000ft above the blinding white saltpan of Badwater, and from this outstanding vista, the valley floor far below indeed looks infernal. The Mesquite Flat Sand Dunes comprise fifteen rippled and contoured square miles of ever-changing sand formations, some over one hundred feet high.

In the northern section of the park, Racetrack Valley Road runs twenty dusty miles from Ubehebe Crater to Teakettle Junction, where visitors hang teakettles, many of them elaborately decorated, on a signpost. Racetrack Valley itself is a 2.5-mile-long mud flat punctuated by the Grandstand, a bizarre black-rock intrusion that breaks up the place's symmetry – small boulders seem slowly to be racing, leaving faint trails in their wake.

Humans have also left their mark here. The remains of the early 20th-century Keane Wonder Mine and Mill includes an aerial tramway, while Scotty's Castle is a grand Spanish Revival style mansion built during the 1920s as the desert retreat of a wealthy Chicago insurance broker.

Ubehebe Crater

Bare trees among the sand dunes

Scotty's Castle

Chuckwalla lizard

Natural stone arches

Rock climbing the Wonderland of Rocks

Lizard

Rock formations

JOSHUA TREE

Covering a vast area where the high Mojave meets the lower Colorado Desert, Joshua Tree National Park is one of the most magical and beguiling of California's national parks. Almost 1250 square miles have been set aside for the park's ragged and gnarled namesakes, which flourish in an otherwise sparsely vegetated landscape. "Joshua Tree" may be a familiar name today, thanks in part to U2's 1987 album, but it isn't, in fact, a tree at all, but a type of yucca. It got its unusual name from Mormons who travelled through the region in the 1850s and imagined the craggy branches to be the arms of Joshua leading them to the Promised Land. Joshua trees are only found in the northwestern quarter of the park, where they form a perfect counterpoint to surreal clusters of monzogranite boulders, great rock piles pushed up from the earth by the movements of the Pinto Mountain Fault running directly below. Often as tall as a hundred feet, the rock edges are rounded and smooth from thousands of years of flash floods and winds, but there are enough nodules, fissures and irregularities to make this superb rock climbing territory. The Wonderland of Rocks area draws climbers from all over the world.

Joshua Tree National Park

Blossoming cholla cactus

Old abandoned mine in Joshua Tree National Park

Keys Ranch in Joshua Tree National Park

Palms at Cottonwood Springs

Other highlights include Keys View, perched on the crest of the Little San Bernardino Mountains, a 5185ft-high vista offering the best views in the whole park. On a good day, you can see as far as the Salton Sea and the snow-covered peak of San Gorgonio Mountain – a brilliant desert panorama of badlands and mountains.

The Cholla Cactus Garden is an astonishing concentration of the "jumping" cholla cactus, as well as creosote bushes, jojoba and several other cactus species. Dusk or dawn is the best chance of seeing the mainly nocturnal desert wood rat. Nearby, the almost barren desert at Ocotillo Patch comes stuffed with spindly ocotillo plants, most attractive in spring for their scarlet blooms.

Cottonwood Spring was used for centuries by the Cahuilla people, and later became an important water stop for prospectors and miners. Ruins of abandoned gold mills can still be seen nearby. Some of the best views in the park are from the top of Ryan Mountain (5461ft), seven hundred strenuous feet above the desert floor.

The park's cultural heritage includes Keys Ranch, once home to tough desert rat and indefatigable miner Bill Keys, a Russian by birth who lived here with his family from 1910 until his death (at age 89) in 1969.

KINGS CANYON

Covering vast swathes of the rugged Sierra Nevada, Kings Canyon National Park contains dizzying mountain scenery, with over 95 percent of the park designated as wilderness (it's also jointly administered with Sequoia National Park). Its key feature is a canyon gored out of the rock by the Kings River, which cascades in torrents down from the High Sierra during the spring snowmelt period.

Cedar Grove huddles at the bottom of Kings Canyon at the start of several hiking trails, notably to lacy Mist Falls and the sapphire blue Rae Lakes. Access is along Hwy-180, which spectacularly skirts – and then dives into – the colossal gorge, by some measurements the deepest canyon in the US at about 7900ft. The canyon's walls of granite and gleaming blue marble are pockmarked white with spectacularly blooming yucca plants (particularly in May and early June). Boyden Cavern (located in Sequoia National Forest, but only accessible from the national park), is home to awe-inspiring stalagmites, stalactites and flowstones – the short but steep hike to the cave offers jaw-dropping views of Kings Canyon.

The main entry point to the park is Grant Grove, set amid concentrated stands of sequoias, sugar pines, incense cedar, black oak and mountain dogwoods. The General Grant Tree has the world's second largest trunk, while you can actually walk through the "Fallen Monarch". The nearby Big Stump Area gets its name, unsurprisingly, from the gargantuan stumps that litter the place – remnants of sequoia logging between 1892 and 1918.

Kings Canyon

SEQUOIA

Located along the western flank of the southern Sierra Nevada, Sequoia National Park boasts the thickest concentration of giant sequoia trees found anywhere in the world. Sparkling streams flow through canyons rimmed with dense forests, while high meadows are freckled with paintbox-hued wildflowers. Giant Forest is the site of the parks' main museum, right in the heart of a grove of enormous trees. From here, Crescent Meadow Road spurs off southeast past Moro Rock, a granite monolith streaking wildly upwards from the green hillside with stunning views from its remarkably level top, and Tunnel Log, a tree that fell across the road in 1937 and has since had a vehicle-sized hole cut through its lower half.

North of Crescent Meadow Road, Generals Highway passes the biggest sequoia of them all: the General Sherman Tree, estimated to be 2300–2700 years old, is 275ft high and has a base diametre of 36.5ft. Its extraordinary dimensions are hard to grasp in the midst of all the other monstrous sequoias here.

The Generals Highway continues northeast to Lodgepole at the end of the Tokopah Valley, with hiking trails leading through deep forests, and longer treks rising above the tree line to reveal the barren peaks and superb vistas of the High Sierra. Twisting Mineral King Road cuts 23 miles across the southern section of Sequoia National Park to Mineral King itself, which sits in a scalloped bowl at 7800ft, surrounded by snowy peaks and glacial lakes.

Giant sequoia trees

Moro Rock, Sequoia National Park

General Sherman Tree

Wild Marmot, Tokopah Valley

Lassen Volcanic National Park

Meadows with trickling streams

Leopard Lily

LASSEN VOLCANIC

Lassen Volcanic National Park, tucked away in a remote corner of the southern Cascade Range, is not just beautiful; it is a geological hotspot, where mudpots bubble and hot springs steam. Lassen also offers opportunities to escape into the wilderness, where your only company is likely to be mule deer, chipmunks and an occasional black bear. With an elevation range of 5000–10,000ft, you can explore a variety of ecological zones in a short period of time, from crystal-clear lakes, wildflower meadows and dense coniferous forests at the lower elevations to the treeless snowfields atop 10,457ft Lassen Peak itself, the southernmost active volcano in the Cascades. In the spring, trails to the summit are sprinkled with wildflowers (violets, irises, lupines and monkeyflowers). From the top there are astonishing views of Mount Shasta to the north and Sutter Butte to the south.

The 30-mile (48km) Lassen Volcanic Park Highway, the park's one paved road, loops around three sides of Lassen Peak and offers access to trails, lakes and geothermal features. Among the park's attractions are the Sulphur Works, where a well-signed boardwalk snakes past sulphurous mudpots and fumaroles; and the Bumpass Hell Trail, with views of deep-blue Lake Helen, impressive glacier-carved rock formations and hemlock trees, as well as the thermal hotspot itself at the end of the trail.

Sunset over Pinnacles National Park

PINNACLES

Encompassing a slice of the Coast Ranges east of the Salinas Valley in Central California, Pinnacles National Park is studded with startling volcanic spires, cool caves and brilliant reds and golds, all set against a perennially clear blue sky. It's best visited in spring (especially March and April), when the air is still cool and the chaparral hillsides are lushly green and sprinkled with wildflowers. Also watch for legions of bees, as this park boasts the highest known bee diversity in the world – some four hundred species in all. Although Pinnacles has east and west entrances, no road transects its steep spires; several paths allow exploration of its wonders from either entrance, however, and Pinnacles' main allure is a day or two spent hiking some of the park's 35 miles of well-maintained trails.

One of the best hikes is the Balconies Trail (two-mile loop; 100ft ascent), most easily accessed from the west, which skirts the multicoloured, 600ft face of the Balconies outcrop, then returns via a series of talus caves formed by huge boulders now wedged between the walls of the narrow canyons. Most of the park's facilities are centred around the more remote eastern entrance, including the Pinnacles Visitor Center and Bear Gulch Nature Center.

Entry sign to the Bear Gulch caves

Bitterroot

Indian paintbrush

Gentle hiking through the national park

Canyon tops

Twisting trees

BLACK CANYON OF THE GUNNISON

Containing a narrow, precipitous gorge a mind-boggling one-mile deep, the Black Canyon of the Gunnison lies deep in the Rockies of western Colorado. The view down into the fearsome, black rock canyon to the foaming Gunnison River below is as mesmerizing as mountain scenery gets. Over two million years, the river has eroded a deep, narrow gorge, leaving exposed cliffs and jagged spires of crystalline rock more than 1.7 billion years old. The one-way, aspen-lined South Rim Road leading through the park to the top of the

canyon winds uphill until the trees abruptly come to an end, the road levels out and the scenery takes a dramatic turn – stark black cliffs, with the odd pine clinging to a tiny ledge. The road is lined with 12 overlooks, including Gunnison Point behind the visitor centre, the Pulpit Rock overlook and Painted View Wall, where the vast scale and height of the streaky cliffs really hits home. South Rim Road ends at High Point (8289ft), and the Warner Point Trail, which cuts through groves of mountain mahogany, serviceberry, pinyon pine and juniper to provide spectacular views of the San Juan Mountains to the south. Rugged North Rim is the quieter, more primitive side of the park, with gravel roads and trails to Exclamation Point and panoramic vistas at Green Mountain.

Great Sand Dunes National Park

GREAT SAND DUNES

Your first sight of Great Sand Dunes National Park comes as a shock; far from being tucked away in crevices or sheltered in a valley, the dunes are a colossal pile of sand that appears to have been dumped alongside the craggy Sangre de Cristo Mountains, 170 miles southwest of Colorado Springs. Over millions of years, these fine glacial grains have eroded from the San Juan Mountains and blown east until they could drift no further; the result is an eerie and deeply incongruous thirty-square-mile area of silky, shifting trackless desert, visible from miles around. The Great Sand Dunes was granted national monument status in 1932, and became a national park in 2004.

The park's visitor centre is three miles beyond the park entrance. Shortly beyond that lies the goal for most visitors, the "beach" beside Medano Creek, which flows along the eastern and southern side of the dune mass. The dunes themselves loom large across the shallow creek (easy to cross on foot). Tough climbs up the giant banks of sand are rewarded by slides back down, freestyle or on sandboards. The scenery is spectacular; the massive 750ft pyramid-shaped peak of Star Dune, the tallest, provides views across the whole park. There are no designated trails in the sand – you can walk wherever you wish. In contrast, the Montville Nature Trail and Mosca Pass Trail weave through aspen and evergreen forests on the edge of the dunes, offering welcome shade in the summer. July is the best month to visit for wildflowers and snowfields sprinkled upon the cliffs.

Medano Creek

Sand boarding the dunes

Mountain peaks

Colourful flora in the park

Buffalo herd

Greater sandhill cranes

Sunflowers in Great Sand Dunes

Frozen Waterfall at Sangre de Cristo Mountains

In the more isolated northern, Sangre de Cristo Mountains section of the park lies Medano Lake, where a challenging trail leads up to Mount Herard (13,297ft) – at the top, awe-inspiring views of the whole dunefield await. Much of the national park comprises grasslands, shrublands and wetlands surrounding the main dunefield on three sides. Herds of elk and bison roam these areas, and millions of prairie sunflowers bloom in mid-August. The easy Sand Sheet Loop Trail provides a small taster of the grassland eco-system, often frequented by miniature short-horned lizards, pronghorns, vesper sparrows and burrowing owls. The San Luis Lakes State Wildlife Area adjacent to the National Park contains wetlands that attract white-faced ibis, American avocets, night herons, snowy egrets, great blue herons and thousands of sandhill cranes in the spring and autumn.

View towards the sand dunes

Kiva Ladder at Spruce Tree House

Cliff Palace

Kiva, a religious room, Cliff Palace

Square Tower

MESA VERDE

The only US national park exclusively devoted to archeological remains, Mesa Verde National Park lies high in the plateaus of southwest Colorado. It's an astonishing place, so far off the beaten track that its extensive Ancestral Puebloan ruins remained unseen by outsiders until late in the nineteenth century. Mesa Verde itself – meaning "green table" in Spanish – is a densely wooded sandstone plateau, cut at its southern edge by sheer canyons that divide the land into narrow fingers. Hundreds of natural alcoves, eaten high into the canyon walls by seeping water, served as homes for over seven hundred years; by the time they were abandoned, around 1300, several held multistorey cliff dwellings that have remained virtually intact to this day.

The park includes several Ancestral Puebloan sites. Spruce Tree House comprises several well-preserved three-storey structures, snugly moulded into the recesses of a rocky alcove and fronted by open plazas. This neat little village was occupied from around 1200 until 1276. One *kiva* (religious building) has been re-roofed, and visitors can enter the dusty, unadorned interior by ladder.

The park's two best-known attractions, Cliff Palace and Balcony House, are on the Cliff Palace Loop Road, and can be explored on guided tours only. Cliff Palace is the largest Ancestral Puebloan cliff dwelling that survives anywhere. Tucked a hundred feet below an overhanging ledge of pale rock, it holds 217 rooms and 23 *kivas*, each thought to have belonged to a separate family or clan. It's thought this was a ceremonial or storage centre rather than simply a communal habitation, and may have been home to around 120 people. Fading murals can still be discerned inside some structures.

Balcony House is one of the few Mesa Verde complexes that was clearly geared towards defence. Built around 1240, it was remodelled during the 1270s to make it even more impregnable. Guided tours involve scrambling up three hair-raising ladders and crawling through a narrow tunnel, above a steep drop into Soda Canyon. It's a spectacular site, with two circular *kivas* standing side by side in a commanding central position.

Mesa Top Loop Road features Square Tower House, an eighty-room alcove complex, focused around the four-storey Square Tower – at 26 feet, the park's tallest tower. Sun Point Overlook looks across Spruce Canyon to as many as twelve distinct cliff dwellings, including Cliff Palace, making it clear just how crowded the canyon was in its heyday. The 12-mile drive onto Wetherill Mesa ends at the Step House, where a single alcove contains a restored pithouse, dating to 626 AD, as well as a pueblo from 1226. Nearby, the park's second-largest ruin, Long House is set in its largest cave; hour-long tours descend sixty or so steps to reach its central plaza, then scramble around its 150 rooms and 21 *kivas*.

Cliff Palace Loop Road

ROCKY MOUNTAIN

The full, pristine grandeur of the Rockies, and especially its wildlife, is preserved within Rocky Mountain National Park in the heart of Colorado. The park straddles the Continental Divide at elevations often well in excess of 10,000ft, with a third of the park above the tree line – large areas of snow never melt. The park's lower reaches hold patches of lush greenery among the rich forests; you never know when you may stumble upon a sheltered mountain meadow flecked with wildflowers.

The showpiece of the park is Trail Ridge Road, the 45-mile stretch of US-34 that connects the small gateway towns of Estes Park and Grand Lake. The highest-elevation paved road in any US national park (cresting at 12,183ft) it affords a succession of tremendous views, and several short trails start from car parks along the way.

Rocky Mountain National Park

Kawuneeche Valley

Odessa Lake

Bull Moose

Bear Lake

Estes Park

American Pika

Starting at Beaver Meadows Visitor Center, the road climbs gently thro-ugh foothills scattered with ponderosa pine and sagebrush. At Deer Ridge Junction, Trail Ridge Road veers left and makes an abrupt ascent along Hidden Valley Creek, dammed in several places by beavers. The creek is also home to rare greenback cutthroat trout. The road passes through stands of fir and Engelmann spruce and then, beyond the stunning overlook at Forest Canyon, enters alpine tundra, a treeless, windblown realm. Pudgy yellow-bellied mar-mots scamper across the road, while bighorn sheep, elk, or mule deer graze warily in distant meadows. Stunted by wind and cold, gnarled whitebark pine hugs the ground, while lupines, yellow snow buttercups, shooting stars, daisies and blue Colorado columbines send a blush through the meadows in late June.

Majestic peaks and alpine tundra are at their most breathtaking to either side of the Alpine Visitor Center, halfway along at Fall River Pass at 11,796ft. The final stretch of Trail Ridge Road descends into Kawuneeche Valley, where conife-rous forests grow thick and the Colorado River is fringed with aspens and willows that explode with autumn colours. Moose and elk are a common sight, and the birdwatching, especially for songbirds such as warblers, thrushes, and finches, is generally excellent.

An alternative scenic drive through the park follows the unpaved, summer-only Old Fall River Road, completed in 1920. Running east–west (one-way) along the bed of a U-shaped glacial valley, it's much quieter than its paved counterpart, and there's far more chance of spotting wildlife. The best launching point for numerous day and overnight hikes is Bear Lake, a pretty spot at the end of a spur road from Estes Park where the mountains are framed to perfection in its cool, still waters.

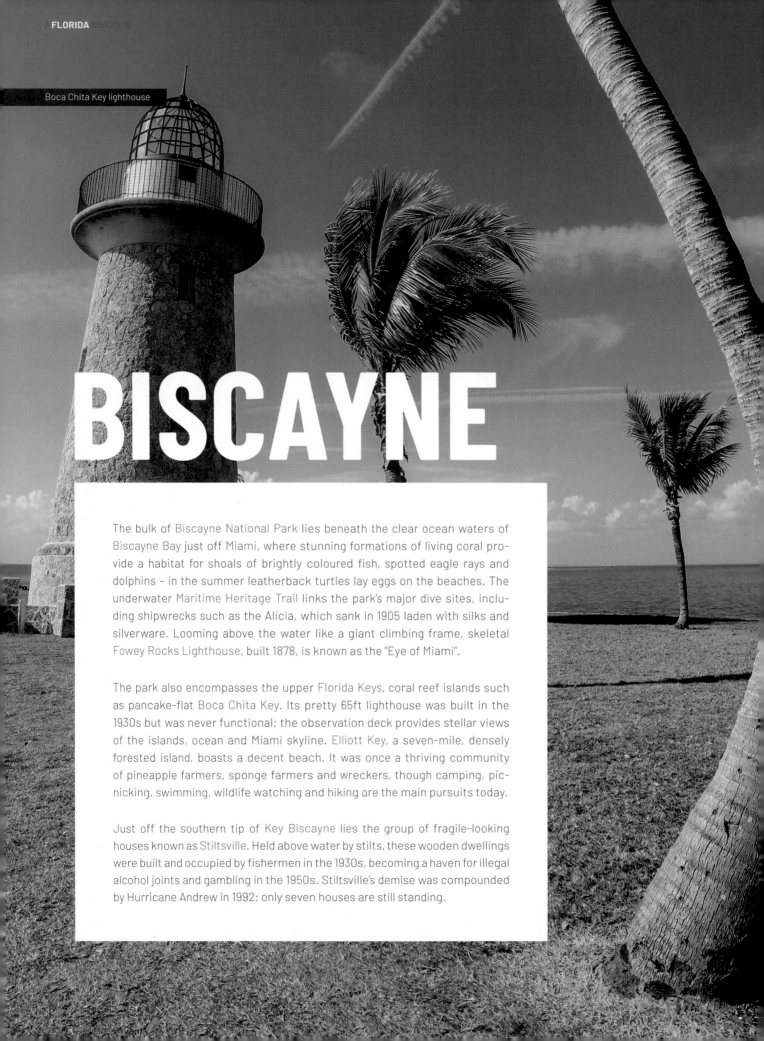

Boca Chita Key lighthouse

BISCAYNE

The bulk of Biscayne National Park lies beneath the clear ocean waters of Biscayne Bay just off Miami, where stunning formations of living coral provide a habitat for shoals of brightly coloured fish, spotted eagle rays and dolphins – in the summer leatherback turtles lay eggs on the beaches. The underwater Maritime Heritage Trail links the park's major dive sites, including shipwrecks such as the Alicia, which sank in 1905 laden with silks and silverware. Looming above the water like a giant climbing frame, skeletal Fowey Rocks Lighthouse, built 1878, is known as the "Eye of Miami".

The park also encompasses the upper Florida Keys, coral reef islands such as pancake-flat Boca Chita Key. Its pretty 65ft lighthouse was built in the 1930s but was never functional; the observation deck provides stellar views of the islands, ocean and Miami skyline. Elliott Key, a seven-mile, densely forested island, boasts a decent beach. It was once a thriving community of pineapple farmers, sponge farmers and wreckers, though camping, picnicking, swimming, wildlife watching and hiking are the main pursuits today.

Just off the southern tip of Key Biscayne lies the group of fragile-looking houses known as Stiltsville. Held above water by stilts, these wooden dwellings were built and occupied by fishermen in the 1930s, becoming a haven for illegal alcohol joints and gambling in the 1950s. Stiltsville's demise was compounded by Hurricane Andrew in 1992; only seven houses are still standing.

Pelican in Biscayne National Park

Coconut palm tree

Wooden dwelling in Stiltsville

Fowey Rocks Lighthouse

Sooty Tern

Dry Tortugas Lighthouse

Cannon in Fort Jefferson

Fort Jefferson remnants

DRY TORTUGAS

Comprising seven small islets deep in the Gulf of Mexico, Dry Tortugas National Park lies some 70 miles west of Key West, accessible only by boat or seaplane. Approaching Garden Key by sea is a magical experience, its weathered stone walls rising up from the ocean like a mirage. Spanish conquistador Juan Ponce de León named the islands for the large numbers of turtles (tortugas in Spanish) he found there in 1513 – the "dry" was added later to warn mariners of the islands' lack of fresh water. Today Garden Key is dominated by Fort Jefferson. Started in 1846 and intended to protect US interests on the Gulf, the fort was never completed, despite thirty years of building. Instead it served as a prison, until intense heat, lack of fresh water, outbreaks of disease, and hurricanes made the fort inoperable – it was abandoned in 1874, its main walls and buildings till intact. Enticing beaches and crystal-clear waters now ring the fort; visibility is normally excellent and schools of fish (and occasionally turtles) laze in the moat and just off the beach and pier.

The park was created in 1992 primarily to protect the nesting grounds of the sooty tern – a black-bodied, white-hooded bird (it's also home to significant colonies of frigate birds and brown noddies). Great flocks of frigate birds are usually visible on nearby Long Key, with sooty terns on Bush Key.

Fort Jefferson from above

Purple Gallinule

Crocodile

Airboat tour

Wild Buttonbush

EVERGLADES

Florida's vast, watery wilderness, the Everglades has a raw but subtle appeal that makes a stark contrast to America's more rugged national parks. The most dramatic sights are small pockets of trees poking above a completely flat sawgrass plain, yet these wide-open spaces resonate with life, forming part of an ever-changing ecosystem. The sawgrass is replenished by water that flows as a wide sheet from Lake Okeechobee to the coast, sustaining a food chain that ends with larger wildlife such as alligators. Where natural indentations in the limestone fill with marl, tree islands – or "hammocks" – appear. Close to hammocks, often surrounding gator holes, are wispy green-leafed willows, pinewoods and - in the deep depressions that hold water the longest - dwarf cypress trees, their treetops forming a distinctive "cypress dome".

From Shark Valley, the sawgrass plain stretches as far as the eye can see, dotted by hardwood hammocks. You won't see any sharks here: the "valley" is actually part of the Shark River Slough, which ends up emptying into Florida Bay. A 15-mile (24km) loop road takes in some of the best wildlife, while a 45-ft (14m) observation tower offers a panoramic overview of the plains.

Cypress trees in the Everglades

Royal Palm is the departure point for two interpretive walks through a section of park known as Pine Island. Alligators are easily spotted along the Anhinga Trail, a boardwalk bordering Taylor Slough. In the winter the reptiles are often splayed right across the path, as motionless as plastic props. Turtles, marsh rabbits and the odd raccoon also frequent the area, as well as the bizarre anhinga, a black-bodied bird resembling an elongated cormorant. In contrast, the Gumbo Limbo Trail is a paved path through a hardwood hammock packed with strangler figs, red-barked gumbo limbos, royal palms, wild coffee and resurrection ferns. The latter appear dead during the dry season, but "resurrect" themselves in the summer rains to form a lush collar of green.

Flamingo, a one-time pioneer fishing colony, is now the gateway to the Florida Bay section of the park. The bay and its adjoining maze of mangrove waterways provide habitats for thousands of birds and a wealth of fish, crabs, shrimp and other marine life. Flamingo is also the southern terminus of the 99-mile (159km) Wilderness Waterway, a marked kayak trail that winds its way to Everglades City. This small town is a base to explore the Ten Thousand Islands, numerous mangrove keys scattered like jigsaw-puzzle pieces along the coastline. Travelling by boat or canoe, expect to see plenty of birds (herons, egrets and fish-feeding pelicans) along the way.

Great Blue Herons

HAWAI'I VOLCANOES

Kīlauea, one of the world's only drive-up volcanoes, is the red-hot heart of Hawai'i Volcanoes National Park. Located on the island of Hawai'i, 'the Big Island', it also happens to be the world's most active volcano, having erupted almost continuously from 1983 to 2018, causing considerable damage. For now, at least, the rivers of lava and towering billows of steam along the coast are no more.

The national park was founded in 1916 to protect the natural wonders of Kīlauea and its fuming neighbour, Mauna Loa volcano. The 505-sq-mile preserve also encompasses sections of the Kalapana Coast, just down slope of Kīlauea itself. The main park highlight is the 11-mile spin around Crater Rim Drive, which skirts the huge steaming craters of Kīlauea Iki, Halema'uma'u and others. Along the way are eerie tree molds formed when a lava flow rushed through the forest, splashed around trees and hardened in their shape. What's left are phantasmagoric black sculptures. Just beyond the Kīlauea Visitor Center are giant steam vents and the trailhead to Sulphur Banks, where pungent volcanic gases seep out of the ground along with groundwater steam. From the Kīlauea Iki Overlook a trail descends through a jungle of tree ferns, then meanders across the floor of an old lava lake crater as sulphurous steam escapes through trailside vents. At the adjacent Thurston Lava Tube, a trail runs through a lava tunnel that once surged with magma.

Kīlauea Iki lava flow

Mauna Loa volcano

Ferns

Pu'u Leo Petroglyphs

Lava flow

Ohia flower

Thurston Lava Tube

Holei Sea Arch

Bird of Paradise

The next overlook provides views of the Pu'u Pua'i cinder cone, while the Devastation Trail runs even closer, cutting through what looks like an utterly barren desert, with skeletons of trees bleached white. Look closer, however, and the trail is studded with tawny grasses, clumps of wildflowers and scarlet 'ōhi'a lehua blossoms, proof of how fast the landscape recovers after eruptions.

Scenic Chain of Craters Road drops down to the coastal section of the park and dead ends at a 1995 lava flow. En route lies Pauahi Crater, which remains culturally significant to the Hawaiian people, who often leave "Hoʻokupu" (offerings wrapped in tī leaf) here. Nearby, the Pu'u Loa Petroglyphs site is another sacred place for Hawaiians, and has been used ritually for over 500 years (it dates between 1200 and 1450). There are more than 23,000 petroglyph images, mostly formed from "pukas" (cup-shaped holes in the rock). At the end of Chain of Craters road, there is a trail to the Pacific Ocean and the captivating Hōlei Sea Arch. The most strenuous trek in the park is the four-day round-trip hike to the top of 13,250ft Mauna Loa, though a shorter but equally demanding round-trip trail to the summit begins at the Mauna Loa Weather Observatory.

"Crater" of Haleakalā volcano

HALEAKALĀ

Haleakalā National Park on the island of Maui protects much of the world's largest dormant volcano. At 10,023ft, Haleakalā, which means "House of the Sun", rises a mile above any other Maui peak. Its "crater" - actually a high, eroded valley between what was two erupting volcanoes and now filled with small cinder cones - is an awesome sight: 21 miles in circumference, 3000ft in depth.

The twisting 11-mile park road provides magnificent views along the crater rim and provides access to the park visitor centre and hiking trails. The Hosmer Grove Nature Walk wriggles through one of the last refuges of the honeycreeper, among the rarest birds in the world. Traversing a precipitous natural land bridge known as "Rainbow Bridge", the Halemau'u Trail descends a series of switchbacks to the crater floor and on through strands of endangered silversword, the rare silver plant that grows only at Haleakalā; its sweet-scented blossoms seem to glow with light. The Keonehe'ehe'e (Sliding Sands) Trail also plunges down to the crater floor via "Pele's Paint Pot". Its vibrantly coloured cinders run from russet red and umber streaked with yellow, purple and red to a pale silver and delicate pea green. The shades change with the angle of the sun, and the effect is electrifying.

In contrast, the coastal Kīpahulu section of the park is located beyond the town of Hana on the famous, winding Hana Highway. Here, the ice-cold Pīpīwai Stream cascades to the sea through 'Ohe'o Gulch in a series of falls and large plunge pools dubbed the "Seven Sacred Pools", surrounded by lush rainforest.

Cinder Cone in Haleakala Crater

Hawaiian Silversword

Hawaiian honeycreeper

Seven Sacred Pools, Hana

Great Marsh

Local fauna

Lupine fields

Dune-protecting signpost

INDIANA DUNES

Hugging over 15 miles of the southern shore of Lake Michigan, either side of the Port of Indiana, Indiana Dunes National Park preserves giant sand dunes formed over thousands of years, as well as wetlands, prairies, meandering rivers and tranquil pine forests. The park is also a rich habitat for rare bird species, and is laced with over 50 miles of trails.

The park coastline is sprinkled with fine beaches, with Central Avenue Beach an especially narrow strip backed by sandy cliffs, and Mount Baldy

Beach dominated by a 126ft-high sand dune. The Portage Lakefront and Riverwalk is an ideal spot to watch for migrating birds in the spring and summer. Behind Dunbar Beach dunes lies the Great Marsh, a large interdunal wetland. Flocks of coots, mallards and wood ducks glide over the wetlands, while green herons stalk and beavers play in the channels. From Dunbar Beach, the Dunes Ridge Trail provides panoramic views of the marshes.

Further inland, trails follow the serene Little Calumet River, through forests of maple, beech, basswood and oak, and across the recently restored Mnoké Prairie for a glimpse of the once vast pre-settlement grasslands. Wildflowers speckle the trails along the river in spring. The Heron Rookery is a hardwood forest set along the East Arm Little Calumet River (herons no longer nest here), home to kingfishers, woodpeckers and a wide variety of warblers.

Boardwalks zigzag the sand dunes

Ferry boats ply the river

Deep caves

Entrance to Mammoth Cave

The Frozen Niagara portion of Mammoth Cave

MAMMOTH CAVE

Set in the hilly country of south central Kentucky, Mammoth Cave National Park encompasses the world's longest known cave system, with more than 400 miles explored. Its labyrinthine passages, domed caverns and eye-popping geological formations were carved by acidic water trickling through limestone, including a fantastical display of stalagmites and stalactites. Nowhere else can you get a better lesson in the totality of darkness and the miracle of light. Usually on a tour, a ranger gathers everyone and, after a warning, switches off the lights. The darkness is sudden, absolute.

A variety of lengthy ranger-guided tours explore various parts of the cave system. Tours usually begin on Broadway, also known as the Main Cave, and lead down to Giant's Coffin, a huge rectangular slab of stone that resembles a sarcophagus. One of the highlights is a huge curtain of flowstone known as Frozen Niagara, its 75ft cascade creating the illusion of foaming waters.

The Bottomless Pit is where cave explorer Stephen Bishop first crossed on a cedar log laid over the seemingly endless drop in the 1840s. The limestone has been rendered silky smooth by visitors squeezing through bottlenecks known as Tall Man's Misery and Fat Man's Misery, while Gothic Avenue is smothered with the autographs of nineteenth-century visitors. The centre of Mammoth Dome rises over 200ft, a giant sinkhole traversed by a steel tower that provides up close views of the "Ruins of Karnak", blocks of rock that look like giant pillars of a temple. Several underground rivers flow through the caves to ultimately empty into the Green River outside, including the Styx and Echo River, famed for its population of uniquely colourless and sightless fish.

Among traces of human occupation are American Indian artefacts, a former salt-petre mine and the remains of an experimental tuberculosis hospital, built in 1843 in the belief that the cool atmosphere of the cave would help clear patients' lungs.

The park's attractions are not all subterranean. The park covers sections of the scenic Green River, as it cuts through densely forested hillsides and jagged limestone cliffs. The river is a major angling destination, rich in bluegill, catfish, bass, perch and other game fish, as well as prime territory for kayaking. Scenic trails lace the surrounding hills, for hikers, bikers and horse-riders, from the river to breezy ridges, gaping sinkholes, natural springs, and the historic cemetrey where former enslaved cave guide, the aforementioned Stephen Bishop, now rests.

Interior of Mammoth Cave

ACADIA

Encompassing most of Mount Desert Island off Maine's Atlantic coast, Acadia National Park is visually stunning, with mountains and lakes for secluded rambling, and wildlife such as seals, beavers and bald eagles. The park gateway is the pretty town of Bar Harbor, which began life as an exclusive resort, summer home to the Vanderbilts and the Astors in the nineteenth century.

The 27-mile Park Loop Road system offers outstanding views of the park's ocean shoreline, coastal forests and mountain silhouettes. Its one-way section passes the Wild Gardens of Acadia, offering a taster of all Mount Desert Island's natural habitats, seasonal blooms and native plants, chirping bird life, and a bubbling spring-fed brook. Nearby Sand Beach is a gorgeous shell-strewn strand bounded by twin headlands of pink granite and surrounded by dense forest. Another popular pitstop is Thunder Cave, which booms an hour or two before high tide thanks to waves pounding into the subterranean rocks – water can spray as high as 40ft. Further along, a trail cuts through groves of spruce to emerge suddenly at Otter Cliff, a precipitous 110ft granite ledge with mesmerizing panoramas of the Acadia coast. In the summer, whales can be seen spouting offshore.

Coastline along Acadia National Park

Charming white bridge and house

Autumn Fall colours in the park

Sailing past Aadia National Park

Bass Harbor Head Lighthouse

Sailboat-filled bay

Southwest Harbor

Aerial view of an island near Acadia National Park

Thunder Hole in Acadia National Park

The crystal-clear waters of Jordan Pond mirror the surrounding mountains, while the network of Carriage Roads that spread out from here were funded by John D. Rockefeller Jr. from 1913 to 1940. The roads (which are off-limits to all motor vehicles) are perfect for cyclists, hikers and horse-riders. Heading back to Bar Harbor, Cadillac Mountain (1530ft) is accessible via a winding, narrow road, ending with sumptuous ocean views at the summit.

To the west, the narrow fjord of Somes Sound almost splits the island in two; on the western side, Bass Harbor Head Lighthouse is the only lighthouse on Mount Desert Island, serving as a picturesque target for hikers though the building itself is still in use and off limits. Mount Desert's most memorable eating experiences are to be found near the many lobster pounds all over the

island – Beal's Lobster Pier in Southwest Harbor serves fresh lobster on a rickety wooden pier. Accessible only by boat, much of Isle au Haut also falls within the park, laced with hiking trails along rocky shorelines, wooded uplands, marshes, bogs and the mile-long freshwater Long Pond.

The far more secluded granite headlands of the Schoodic Peninsula, the only part of the park on the mainland, are anchored by Winter Harbor, where a one-way road loops along the shore. Viewpoints on route provide awe-inspiring views of Mount Desert Island, bobbing lobster boats, wheeling gulls and forest-smothered islets out in the mist.

Chippewa Harbour, Isle Royale

ISLE ROYALE

The 45-mile sliver of Isle Royale National Park, fifty miles out in Lake Superior, is geographically and culturally very, very far from urban America. All cars are banned on this blissfully undeveloped enclave, and instead of freeways, 166 miles of hiking trails lead past windswept trees, swampy lakes, paddling loons and grazing moose. The only traces of human life here are ancient mineworks, possibly two millennia old, shacks left behind by commercial fishermen in the 1940s, and a few lighthouses and park buildings. Hiking, canoeing, fishing and scuba-diving among shipwrecks are the principal leisure activities.

The park headquarters is actually located in Houghton on the mainland, though two small visitor centres operate on the island itself, at Rock Harbor and at Windigo, usually open in July and August only. Rock Harbor sits at the northeast end of the island, surrounded by forests of spruce, birch and fir. Out in the harbour sits tiny Raspberry Island, laced with planked trails through the woods and bogs here, home to the rare insect-eating sundew and pitcher plants. Windigo lies on the southwest coast of Isle Royale, at the end of secluded Washington Harbor. From here, trails also fan out through the boreal forest and hills, while crested merganser ducks, otters and moose all reside in and around the water.

Rock Harbor Lighthouse

Beaver swimming at Isle Royale

Moskey Basin

Snowshoe Hare

Grouse in Voyageurs National Park

Ellsworth Rock Gardens

Canoeing in Voyageurs National Park

Water lilies

VOYAGEURS

Set along the border between Minnesota and Canada, Voyageurs National Park is a dazzling maze of interconnected lakes and water highways. Unsurprisingly, this park is best explored by boat, not car. Once out on the lakes, you're in a great, silent world. Kingfishers, osprey and eagles swoop down for their share of the abundant walleye; moose and bear stalk the banks. Cruises depart the Kabetogama and Rainy Lake visitor centres, while during the freeze-up – usually from December until March – the park becomes a prime destination for skiers and snowmobilers.

Highlights include the white granite cliffs of Anderson Bay, providing sensational views across Rainy Lake, and the similarly vertiginous bluffs of Grassy Bay, rising some 125ft above Sand Point Lake.

On the northern shore of Lake Kabetogama, Jack Ellsworth began creating the Ellsworth Rock Gardens in the 1940s, using the natural Minnesota landscape to create unique sculpture and flower terraces backed by dense forest. To the southeast, the shores of Hoist Bay preserve relics from early 20th century logging camps and 1930s resorts. Only accessible by boat or float plane, historic Kettle Falls Hotel was built between 1910 and 1913, when construction of the Kettle Falls dam began.

Lake Kabetogama

The Old Courthouse

Aerial view of the Gateway Arch entrance

Getting up close at Gateway Arch

The glittering gateway

GATEWAY ARCH

An astonishing feat of engineering, the Gateway Arch dominates downtown St Louis; a glittering arc of steel, its vast size is hard to appreciate until you get up close. Designed by Finnish-born architect Eero Saarinen and completed in 1965, the 630ft-high stainless-steel parabola commemorates the role of St Louis in the western expansion of the USA, especially honouring the epic Lewis and Clark Expedition, which set off from here in 1804.

The four-minute "Tram Ride to the Top" shoots up the hollow, gently curving arch to the Observation Deck, where the views of St Louis, the Mississippi and the surrounding tree-studded plains are spectacular. Below the arch lies the interactive Museum at the Gateway Arch, with six themed galleries spanning the history of St Louis and westward expansion 1764 to 1965. The Tucker Theater screens documentary "Monument to the Dream". One-hour Mississippi cruises aboard replica paddlewheelers depart the levee below the Arch.

The park also administers the nearby Old Courthouse, a grand example of the wealth and prestige of St Louis in the nineteenth century. The Greek Revival-style interior contains exhibits charting the development of the city from 1764 to the present day, but the most poignant section is dedicated to the watershed Dred Scott trial that opened here in 1846; the US Supreme Court's decision to rule against Scott eleven years later – effectively sanctioning slavery – helped move the country toward the Civil War.

GLACIER

Two thousand lakes, a thousand miles of rivers, thick forests, breezy meadows and awe-inspiring peaks make up one of America's finest attractions, Glacier National Park – a haven for bighorn sheep, mountain goats, black and grizzly bears, wolves and mountain lions. Although the park does hold 25 small (and rapidly retreating) glaciers, it really takes its name from the huge floes of ice that carved these immense valleys twenty thousand years ago. In the summer months, this is prime hiking and whitewater rafting territory, while huckleberries litter the slopes in autumn.

The 50-mile Going-to-the-Sun Road across the heart of the park is one of the most mesmerizing drives in the country, and driving it from west to east can take several hours – each successive hairpin brings a new colossus into view. Beginning at West Glacier, the road runs east along ten-mile Lake McDonald before starting to climb, as snowmelt from waterfalls gushes across the road, and the winding route nudges over the Continental Divide at Logan Pass (6680ft).

View above Going-to-the-Sun Road

St Mary Lake

The most popular trail in the park begins here, following a boardwalk for a mile and a half across wild-flower-strewn alpine meadows framed by towering craggy peaks, en route to serene Hidden Lake. The highway continues to an overlook at Jackson Glacier, one of the few glaciers visible from the roadside. From here the road descends to St Mary Lake and the east park entrance at St Mary, right on the edge of the Great Plains.

Other more remote sections of the park can be explored by car, bike or on foot, beginning with Many Glacier, anchored by historic Many Glacier Hotel on pristine

Swiftcurrent Lake. From here an easy two-mile loop trail runs along the lake-shore, while a more challenging five-mile, one-way trail heads to Iceberg Lake, so called for the blocks of ice that float on its surface even in midsummer. Another popular option is to take a trip to the foot of the Grinnell Glacier via two boat trips and two hikes.

US-2 runs around the southern border of the park, for 85 miles between West Glacier and St Mary. It's not as dramatic as Going-to-the-Sun Road, but still very scenic; it passes Goat Lick Overlook, a good place to spot mountain goats, the remote village of East Glacier Park and the entrance to the Two Medicine section of the park, a less crowded centre for hiking and boating.

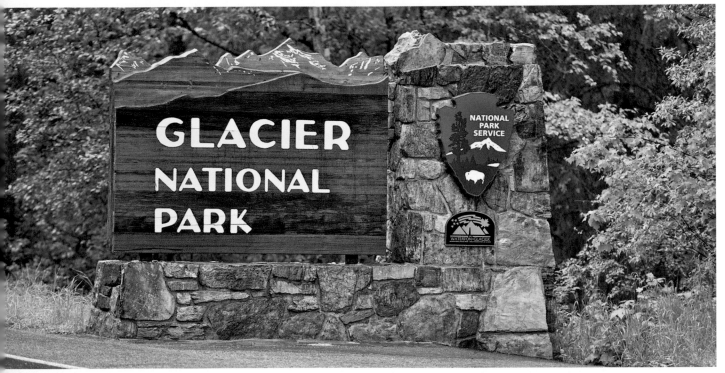

Glacier National Park welcome sign

ighorn sheep

Cracker Lake

Wheeler Peak

Lehman Caves

Bristlecone pine tree

Clear alpine lakes in Great Basin National Park

Colourful flora

GREAT BASIN

The Great Basin lies between the Wasatch Range in Utah and the Sierra Nevada in California, a mostly high, cold desert of grassland and sagebrush. Great Basin National Park in east-central Nevada also contains the cool, green Snake Range: terrestrial islands separated by oceans of sagebrush desert. Some 8000ft of vertical relief separates the valley floor from the summit of 13,063ft Wheeler Peak, the second-highest point in Nevada.

Beneath the mountains lies Lehman Caves, actually a single cavern, carved out of the earth by ground water over millions of years and now 'decorated'

with fascinating limestone formations. Above ground, the 12-mile Wheeler Peak Scenic Drive starts out amid sagebrush, prickly-pear cactus and juniper trees, then enters a zone of pinyon pine and curl-leaf mountain mahogany. As elevation changes, dwarf pinyon woodland cedes to cool aspen forest. Still higher up, stately, loden--hued evergreens – Douglas fir, white fir and Engelmann spruce – begin to appear along with limber pine and 5000-year-old bristlecone pine. The scenic drive ends at an elevation of 10,000ft. The air here is crisp and filled with piney fragrance. Several trails lead to clear alpine lakes, a bristlecone grove, Wheeler Peak Glacier, or the top of Wheeler Peak itself, where the views are sensational: more mountains interrupt the valleys in all directions, like battleships plowing through the sea.

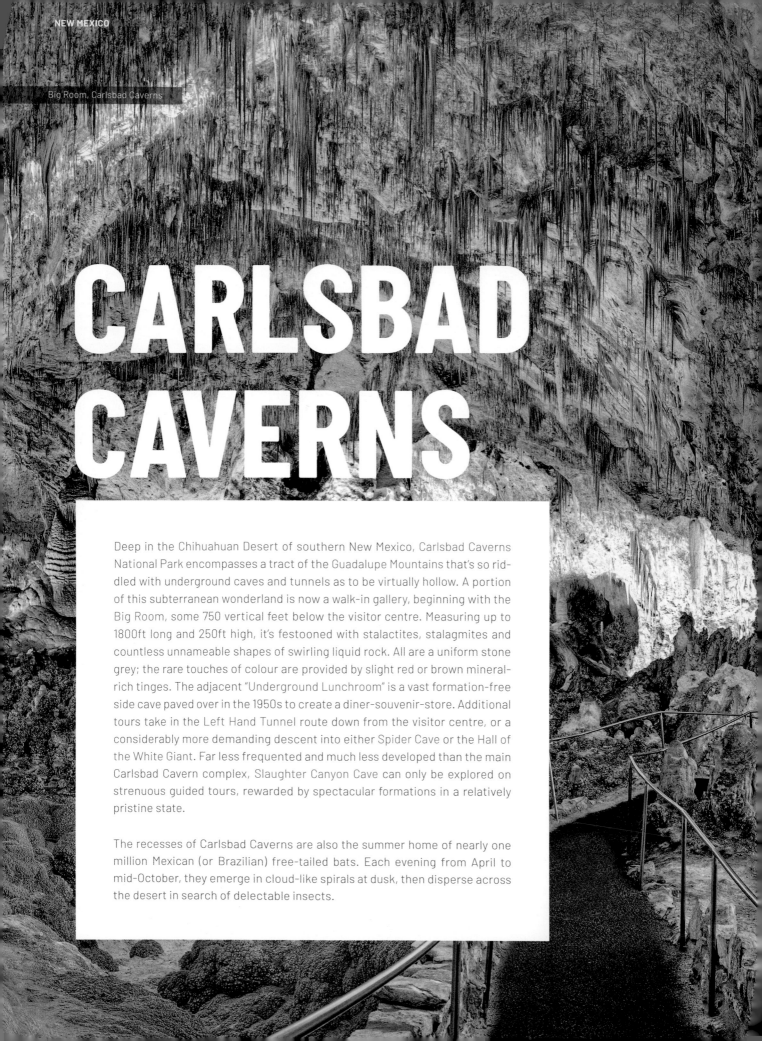

Big Room, Carlsbad Caverns

CARLSBAD CAVERNS

Deep in the Chihuahuan Desert of southern New Mexico, Carlsbad Caverns National Park encompasses a tract of the Guadalupe Mountains that's so riddled with underground caves and tunnels as to be virtually hollow. A portion of this subterranean wonderland is now a walk-in gallery, beginning with the Big Room, some 750 vertical feet below the visitor centre. Measuring up to 1800ft long and 250ft high, it's festooned with stalactites, stalagmites and countless unnameable shapes of swirling liquid rock. All are a uniform stone grey; the rare touches of colour are provided by slight red or brown mineral-rich tinges. The adjacent "Underground Lunchroom" is a vast formation-free side cave paved over in the 1950s to create a diner-souvenir-store. Additional tours take in the Left Hand Tunnel route down from the visitor centre, or a considerably more demanding descent into either Spider Cave or the Hall of the White Giant. Far less frequented and much less developed than the main Carlsbad Cavern complex, Slaughter Canyon Cave can only be explored on strenuous guided tours, rewarded by spectacular formations in a relatively pristine state.

The recesses of Carlsbad Caverns are also the summer home of nearly one million Mexican (or Brazilian) free-tailed bats. Each evening from April to mid-October, they emerge in cloud-like spirals at dusk, then disperse across the desert in search of delectable insects.

Stalactite formations

Soaptree Yucca

Stalacite and stalagmite formations

Dry landscapes near Carlsbad Caverns

White Sands National Park

Snow-like sands

Flora in the desert

WHITE SANDS

Otherworldly enough to double as David Bowie's home planet in *The Man Who Fell To Earth*, the dazzling dunes of White Sands fill 275 square miles of southern New Mexico. Deposited on an ancient seabed 250 million years ago, they're not in fact sands but fine gypsum. Anywhere else, they would have dissolved and been carried off by rivers; here, there are none. The Spanish Pueblo-style adobe Visitor Center was completed in the 1930s, and today houses exhibits and shows *A Land in Motion* film.

Dunes Drive, an eight-mile scenic road, runs from the visitor centre into the heart of the dunefield – the last three miles are a hard-packed, gypsum track. Driving in, you enter a bizarre world of knife-edge ridges and graceful slopes.

Roadside pull-outs, equipped with fabulous 1950s-style curving picnic shelters, enable you to leave your vehicle and wade through glistening sand to the top of the ridges, before slipping and sliding back down. Sledding is permitted in the loop portion of Dunes Drive – waxed, plastic "snow-saucers" can be purchased at the park gift shop. The flora and fauna of the region is introduced on the Dune Life Nature Trail, an easy, one-mile self-guided loop – though the environment appears unforgivingly hostile, Kit foxes, badgers, birds, rodents, and reptiles all live here.

To add to the sense of mystery, this remote region holds the active White Sands Missile Range– the first-ever atomic bomb was detonated here in July 1945 – and road access closes for short periods during tests.

Sunrise over Theodore Roosevelt National Park

Bentonite clay formations

American bison crossing the Scenic Drive Loop

Roaming deer

THEODORE ROOSEVELT

A vast tract of multihued rock formations, rough grass-land and badlands, Theodore Roosevelt National Park is North Dakota's unspoiled wilderness, named after the adventurer and future president who roamed, hunted and ranched here in the 1880s. Split into North and South units along the banks of the Little Missouri River, approximately 70 miles apart, the park is at its most beautiful at sunrise or sundown – the best times to observe mule deer, feral horses, elk, pronghorn, ever-present bison and closely knit prairie dog communities.

Little Missouri River

Cannonball concretions

Theodore Roosevelt National Park welcome sign

Theodore Roosevelt's Maltese Cross Cabin

Prairie Dog

At the main entrance to the park, the Medora Visitor Center contains a small museum dedicated to Theodore Roosevelt; behind it sits the simple Maltese Cross Cabin that served as Roosevelt's first home in North Dakota in 1884. From here, the remarkably scenic 36-mile loop road passes several sprawling prairie dog towns and overlooks. The most spectacular is the view from Wind Canyon, 10 miles out of Medora, where a small gorge of caramel-like sandstone has been shaped smooth by the wind, and the Little Missouri makes a picturesque oxbow in the valley below. Hiking trails lace the park; the Petrified Forest Loop leads to a vast collection of petrified wood and tree stumps. Other highlights of the South Unit include the jaw-dropping Painted Canyon, 7 miles (11km) east of Medora. Here, the land is like a sedimentary layer cake that has been beaten by hard rains for millions of years, baked by the sun into a kaleidoscope of colours, and cut through to its base by the river.

Tiny Medora itself is the southern gateway to the park, a resort town that hums with activity between June and September during the "Medora Musical". This song-and-dance variety show is staged beneath the stars in a marvellously sited amphitheatre, on a hillside just outside town. The extravaganza is preceded by the Pitchfork Steak Fondue, a fantastic feed for which hundreds of steaks are simultaneously dipped on pitchforks into giant oil vats.

The park's smaller North Unit (just 15 miles south of oil-boom town Watford City), receives only a fraction of the South Unit's visitors, though it's arguably more spectacular. Highlights include the jaw-dropping views from River Bend Overlook, along the park's 14-mile scenic drive, and similar vistas from Oxbow Overlook, at the road's end, while the demanding 12-mile Buckhorn Trail winds through sage-filled terrain before following steep gulches up into lofty prairies full of grazing bison.

CUYAHOGA VALLEY

Covering the bucolic landscape along the Cuyahoga River between Akron and Cleveland in northeast Ohio, Cuyahoga Valley National Park encompasses dense forests, rolling hills and open farmland. Around 100 waterfalls are located in the valley, from the plunging Brandywine Falls, the tallest at 65ft, to the more delicate Blue Hen Falls, a lacy 15ft drop within lovely green woods.

Over 125 miles of hiking trails lace the park, most notably the 19.5-mile Towpath Trail, which shadows a now tranquil stretch of the old Ohio and Erie Canal. Constructed parallel to the Cuyahoga River between 1825 and 1832, the canal stopped functioning after the Great Flood of 1913. The park administers several historic properties along the canal, beginning with the Canal Exploration Center at Lock 38. This venerable clapboard structure has served as tavern, store, boarding house and blacksmith shop, assuming its current appearance in the 1850s. Further south, the Boston Mill Visitor Center occupies a white clapboard storehouse built around 1836.

The southern section of the park contains Beaver Marsh, a wildlife and bird rich wetland environment created by beavers that moved in along remnants of the old canal. A boardwalk snakes through the marsh, now smothered in reeds, emerald green water lilies and the stumps of old poplars, cottonwoods, willows and beeches.

Brandywine Falls

CRATER LAKE

Oregon's only national park is centred on a wall of volcanic cliffs encircling a lake of indescribable blue. The blown-out shell of Mount Mazama holds the hypnotically beautiful Crater Lake, formed after an explosion 42 times greater than that of Mount St Helens. Snow and rain blowing in from the Pacific took about 800 years to fill the caldera, which – at a depth of 1943ft – now contains the deepest freshwater lake in the US. The caldera is ringed with a blanket of conifers that drop to the water's edge and envelop the mountain in every direction but north, where the ash-smothered Pumice Desert remains stark and treeless.

The lake is encircled by a dizzying 33-mile road known as Rim Drive, which is punctuated by numerous scenic overlooks and trailheads. From the road, a steep, 2.5-mile trail climbs to the summit of 8929ft Mount Scott, the park's highest peak. The path makes a switchback ascent through dense stands of subalpine fir and clusters of wildflowers before rising above timberline, where gnarled whitebark pine eke out an existence. Mount Scott is the finest visual perch in the park. Here red-tailed hawks, golden eagles and other raptors soar on the air currents that curl up the mountain like invisible waves.

A hammock with a view

Ground Squirrel

Vidae Falls

Pumice Castle

Sunrise at Crater Lake National Park

Hazy view across the lake towards the National Park

Crater Lake welcome sign

Phantom Ship volcanic dyke

Steller's Jay

Beyond the Mount Scott trailhead, a spur road leads to Cloudcap, the highest overlook on the rim, where you can get good views of the Phantom Ship, a jagged volcanic dyke poking through the lake surface that, in dim light or fog, resembles a mysterious clipper on the water.

Further along the rim, the Castle Crest Wildflower Garden Trail offers a half-mile stroll through a medley of blossoming flowers during the summer months. A variety of hummingbirds summer in this area, and you can often see or hear them zipping through the underbrush. The most prominent landmark on the lake itself is Wizard Island, the tip of a still-rising cinder cone soaring 700ft above water level like a wizard's cap. The Wizard Island Overlook offers the best view. Tour boats run out to Wizard Island from Cleetwood Cove on the northeast lakeshore, connected to Cleetwood Cove Overlook on the rim via an extremely steep mile-long trail. On the lake, cormorants and gulls skim the water, bald eagles circle the cliffs, and a variety of waterfowl bob peacefully on the surface. On the island, the fairly strenuous Wizard Island Summit Trail leads about a mile to its dormant crater.

Cypress forest in Congaree National Park

CONGAREE

Set in central South Carolina, Congaree National Park protects the largest intact expanse of old growth bottomland hardwood forest in the US. The Congaree River flows through the park, its waters nourishing the lowland floodplain forest. Some of the tallest trees in the country grow here, including a 167ft loblolly pine, towering sweetgum, cherrybark oak, American elm, swamp chestnut oak and common persimmon. The forest also harbours plenty of wildlife, from bobcats, deer, feral pigs and raccoons to armadillos, wild turkeys and otters.

Hiking trails fan out across the wetlands. The Boardwalk Loop cuts an elevated 2.4-mile walkway through a forest of soaring bald cypress and tupelo trees, oaks, maples and holly. The Weston Lake Loop Trail wriggles along Cedar Creek where otters and wading birds can be seen, while the Oakridge Trail traverses a ridge lined with large oak trees and low-lying sloughs frequented by deer. The River Trail meanders along the Congaree for 10.4 miles, where large sandbars emerge when the water is low and the vegetation is far denser than on other trails. The marked Cedar Creek Canoe Trail snakes for 15 miles through the forest, from Bannister's Bridge to the Congaree River, with large bald cypress trees on either bank forming a natural canopy over the sluggish waters. Old logs provide perches for snakes and turtles, while river otters and the occasional alligator weave through the creek.

Section of the Boardwalk Loop

Resident insects in the National Park

Snake in a moss-lined tree

Bald Cypress Knees

Pronghorn antelope

Section of a walking trail

Sunset over the Badlands

Wigwams against a rainbow mountain backdrop

BADLANDS

Located in southwestern South Dakota, the spectacularly eroded layers of sand, ash, mud and gravel in Badlands National Park were created over 35 million years ago, when there was an ancient sea here. The sea subsequently dried up; over the last few million years, erosion has slowly eaten away at the terrain revealing mesmerizing gradations of earth tones and pastel colours. The crumbly earth is carved into all manner of shapes: pinnacles, precipices, pyramids, knobs, cones, ridges and gorges looming out of the desert like lunar sandcastles and cathedrals. The rainbow hues that colour these formations are most striking at dawn, dusk and just after rainfall (heaviest in May and June). The park also protects an expanse of mixed grass prairie where bison, bighorn sheep, prairie dogs and black-footed ferrets live today.

Badlands National Park

Bighorn sheep

Driving the Badlands Loop Road

South Dakota Badlands

Western bluebird

Rainbow-striped rock formations

The Badlands Loop Road, also known as Highway-240, slices through the North Unit of the park, beginning on the eastern side with the Big Badlands Overlook, a dizzying vista of multi-hued, jagged rocks. Nearby, the Door Trail follows a short boardwalk into an otherworldly wasteland of crumbling white rock pinnacles, while the Notch Trail cuts a more strenuous route through a canyon and up a log ladder before ending at a ledge with a stunning view of the White River Valley. Across the road, the gently undulating Castle Trail snakes through spires, buttes and prairies for over 5 miles one-way, along the north edge of the Badland Wall.

Just before the Ben Reifel Visitor Center, the Loop Road passes the Cliff Shelf Trailhead, where a boardwalk cuts a short loop through juniper forest along the Badlands Wall. Further along, the short Fossil Exhibit Trail is lined with replica fossils and displays on the now-extinct creatures that once lived here. Continuing into the northwest, the Bigfoot Pass Overlook provides some of the most beautiful views in the park, while the Yellow Mounds Overlook takes in a view of vast hills of yellow and russet red fossilized soils.

The South Unit of the park (aka Stronghold District) comprises lands on the Pine Ridge Indian Reservation, managed jointly by the National Park Service and by the Oglala Sioux Tribe. It's a far wilder, rarely visited swathe of badlands and prairie, anchored by the White River Visitor Center. Sheep Mountain Table Road is one of the few tracks into the unit, running 7 miles over rough gravel and ending at a spectacular mesa top overlooking the southern badlands.

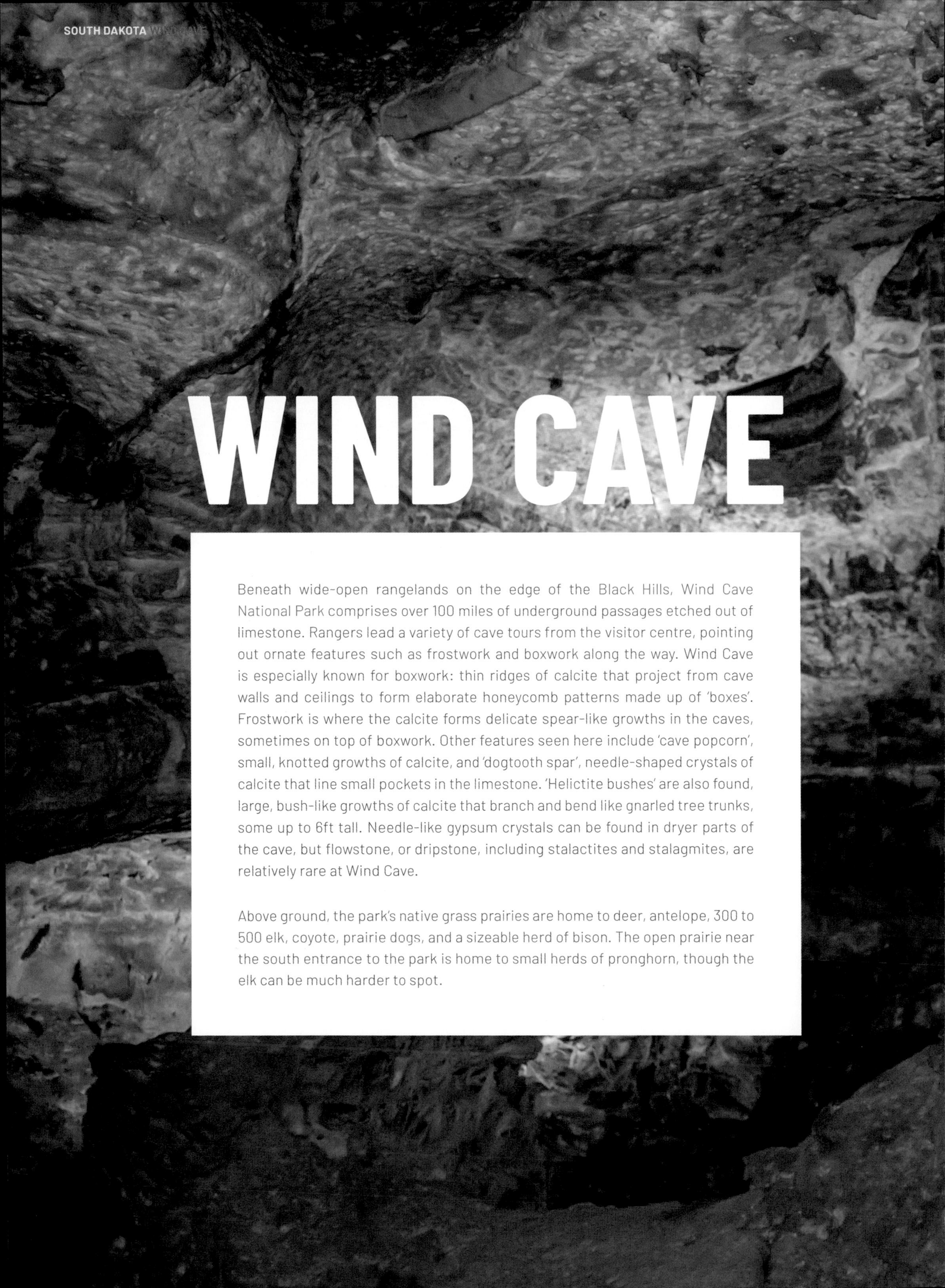

WIND CAVE

Beneath wide-open rangelands on the edge of the Black Hills, Wind Cave National Park comprises over 100 miles of underground passages etched out of limestone. Rangers lead a variety of cave tours from the visitor centre, pointing out ornate features such as frostwork and boxwork along the way. Wind Cave is especially known for boxwork: thin ridges of calcite that project from cave walls and ceilings to form elaborate honeycomb patterns made up of 'boxes'. Frostwork is where the calcite forms delicate spear-like growths in the caves, sometimes on top of boxwork. Other features seen here include 'cave popcorn', small, knotted growths of calcite, and 'dogtooth spar', needle-shaped crystals of calcite that line small pockets in the limestone. 'Helictite bushes' are also found, large, bush-like growths of calcite that branch and bend like gnarled tree trunks, some up to 6ft tall. Needle-like gypsum crystals can be found in dryer parts of the cave, but flowstone, or dripstone, including stalactites and stalagmites, are relatively rare at Wind Cave.

Above ground, the park's native grass prairies are home to deer, antelope, 300 to 500 elk, coyote, prairie dogs, and a sizeable herd of bison. The open prairie near the south entrance to the park is home to small herds of pronghorn, though the elk can be much harder to spot.

Boxwork geological formations in Wind Cave National Park

GREAT SMOKY MOUNTAINS

Stretching for 70 miles along the Tennessee–North Carolina border, Great Smoky Mountains National Park lies at the southern end of the Appalachians. These spectacularly corrugated peaks are named for the bluish haze that hangs over them, comprising moisture and hydrocarbons released by the lush vegetation – the park is home to the largest swathe of old-growth forest left standing in the east, and is one of the most biodiverse places on earth. Sixteen peaks rise above 6000ft, their steep elevation accounting for dramatic changes in climate. In spring the high meadows are smothered in wild flowers, while autumn sees the hills shrouded in a canopy of red, yellow and bronze. During June and July, rhododendrons blaze fiercely in the summer heat.

Great Smoky Mountains National Park

John P Cable Grist Mills

Clingman's Dome

Ramsey Cascades

View of the Smoky Mountains from Route 441

Smoky Mountain Tunnel

Young black bear

US-441, known here as the Newfound Gap Road, cuts through the centre of the park from Cherokee to Gatlinburg. The road climbs approximately 3,000ft, ascending through cove hardwood, pine-oak and northern hardwood forest to attain the evergreen spruce-fir forest at Newfound Gap itself. At an elevation of 5,046ft, this is the lowest drivable pass through the national park and is significantly cooler than the surrounding lowlands – it also receives much more snow. From the gap, a spur road winds for seven more miles up to Clingman's Dome, the highest point in Tennessee at 6643ft. A spiral walkway observation tower on top affords a panoramic view of the mountains.

On the northern edge of the park, Roaring Fork Motor Nature Trail winds its way past gurgling mountain streams, old-growth forest, historic log cabins and grist mills. The Noah "Bud" Ogle Cabin is a typically rough-hewn nineteenth--century homestead, close to the trailhead for Rainbow Falls, a lacy cascade

over a huge rock ledge in the heart of the forest. Further east, Ramsey Cascades is the tallest waterfall in the park and one of the most spectacular, plunging some 100ft over a series of rocky outcrops.

Cades Cove lies in the northwest sector of the park, a broad, verdant valley surrounded by mountains. The 11-mile driving loop here passes deserted barns, homesteads, mills and churches that stand as a reminder of the farmers who carved out a living from this wilderness before National Park status was conferred in 1934. White-tailed deer are frequently seen, and sightings of black bear, coyote, groundhog, turkey, raccoon, skunk and other animals are also possible.

Big Bend National Park

BIG BEND

Big Bend Country is a dramatic land of contrasts where island-like mountains and deeply etched canyons break up a vast expanse of the Chihuahuan Desert. Named for a great looping curve in the Rio Grande, Big Bend National Park is starkly beautiful. Cactus, ocotillo and greasewood provide sparse cover in the lowlands, and agave and lechuguilla rise like daggers from the desert floor. At the centre of the park, the Chisos Mountains climb to more than 7800ft, an oasis of cool breezes and shady woodlands. To the south, the Rio Grande courses through the spectacular gorges of Boquillas and Santa Elena canyons, with walls up to 1500ft high.

Big Bend is particularly known as a paradise for birds. The endangered peregrine falcon can still be seen here, as can gray hawks, zone-tailed hawks and black hawks. At dusk, some 20 species of bats swoop through the air, hunting insects. Mule deer can be found in the desert surrounding the Chisos Mountains, and a few fleet-footed pronghorn still roam the flatlands.

Unique rock stack formations

Pink cactus

The Rio Grande river

Giant Dagger Yucca

Strawberry Cactus

Trans-pecos rat snake

Santa Elena Canyon

Yellow cactus flowers

Driving into the Chisos Mountains the desert scrub gives way to a belt of grassland and then scattered savannah-like forest. The road crests at Panther Pass, breaches an outer wall of peaks, and then makes a winding descent into the Chisos Basin – an open, mountain-rimmed valley scattered with a relict woodland of Arizona cypress, Douglas fir, quaking aspen, ponderosa and bigtooth maple. Lush grasses smother the valley floor and mountain slopes, interspersed with thorny patches of cactus. The road dead-ends at the foot of 7550ft Casa Grande Peak, where Boulder Meadow Trail is an easy 3-mile round-trip through pinyon-juniper woodland to a beautiful upland meadow.

Halfway between the park's western and eastern entrances, the Ross Maxwell Scenic Drive runs south to Santa Elena Canyon. The road passes Castolon, where a dusty army garrison was manned between 1914 and 1918 to protect settlers from Mexican bandits – it's now a visitor centre. From here the scenic drive parallels the Rio Grande for about 8 miles before coming to a dead end. A short trail leads into Santa Elena Canyon, where 1500ft limestone cliffs tower over the muddy river.

The 24-mile drive from Panther Junction to Rio Grande Village passes around the eastern flank of the Chisos Mountains. A dirt road branches off to the Hot Springs Historic Area, once a thermal spa resort and still home to natural hot springs that bubble out of the ground. At the end of the main road, cottonwood trees fringe the river at Rio Grande Village, while Boquillas Canyon Overlook boasts stellar views across to Mexico.

Chisos Basin, Big Bend National Park

Agave harvardiana

Sage Thrasher

Hiking trail in the Guadalupe Mountains

Yucca plants

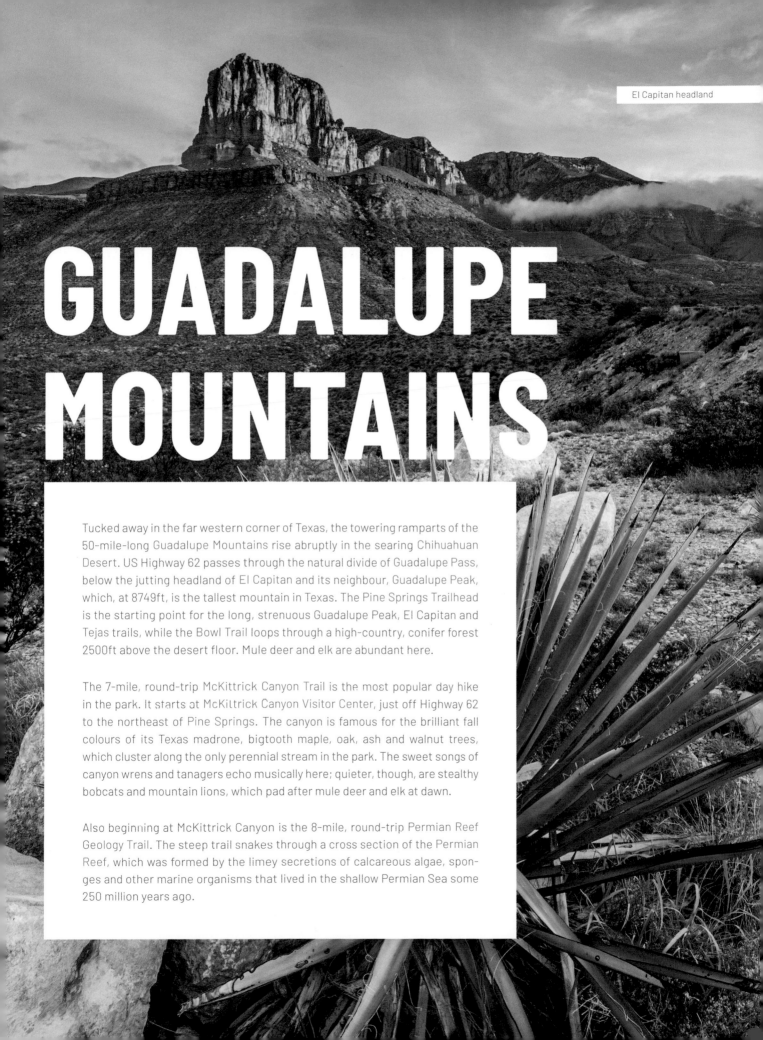

GUADALUPE MOUNTAINS

Tucked away in the far western corner of Texas, the towering ramparts of the 50-mile-long Guadalupe Mountains rise abruptly in the searing Chihuahuan Desert. US Highway 62 passes through the natural divide of Guadalupe Pass, below the jutting headland of El Capitan and its neighbour, Guadalupe Peak, which, at 8749ft, is the tallest mountain in Texas. The Pine Springs Trailhead is the starting point for the long, strenuous Guadalupe Peak, El Capitan and Tejas trails, while the Bowl Trail loops through a high-country, conifer forest 2500ft above the desert floor. Mule deer and elk are abundant here.

The 7-mile, round-trip McKittrick Canyon Trail is the most popular day hike in the park. It starts at McKittrick Canyon Visitor Center, just off Highway 62 to the northeast of Pine Springs. The canyon is famous for the brilliant fall colours of its Texas madrone, bigtooth maple, oak, ash and walnut trees, which cluster along the only perennial stream in the park. The sweet songs of canyon wrens and tanagers echo musically here; quieter, though, are stealthy bobcats and mountain lions, which pad after mule deer and elk at dawn.

Also beginning at McKittrick Canyon is the 8-mile, round-trip Permian Reef Geology Trail. The steep trail snakes through a cross section of the Permian Reef, which was formed by the limey secretions of calcareous algae, sponges and other marine organisms that lived in the shallow Permian Sea some 250 million years ago.

ARCHES

Just north of the Colorado River in eastern Utah, Arches National Park contains a world-renowned ensemble of carved, salmon-coloured arches, fins, spires, pinnacles and balanced rocks. This desert park, 5 miles north of Moab, is home to more than 2000 natural arches and many other strangely eroded red rock giants. Immediately beyond the visitor centre, the park road begins its 18-mile journey north to Devil's Garden with a steep climb up the cliffs. The first stop is Park Avenue, named for the "skyscrapers" that top the high ridges to either side of a dry wash. The trail here skirts a dramatic orange fin before leading to a group of chunky monoliths known as the Courthouse Towers.

In the heart of the park, the extraordinary, 50ft Balanced Rock rests precariously on its slanted pedestal. Immediately beyond, a spur road leads to the Windows Section. A loop trail ambles gently upwards towards North Window, a gaping aperture in the rock framing blue sky and – up close – a magnificent desert panorama.

North Window, Arches National Park

A remarkable free-standing crescent of rock, Delicate Arch – a symbol of Utah – can only be reached via the demanding Delicate Arch Trail. The trail is just 1.5 miles long, but the round-trip involves a steep climb across bare slickrock. The terrain is surprisingly varied, from the scrubby riverbanks, choked with tamarisk, by way of a small-scale piñon-juniper forest, up to the naked rock three-quarters of a mile up. Suddenly, you're confronted by the full glory of Delicate Arch. Standing in superb isolation on the high lip of a canyon, it looks much taller than its 45ft. At sunset, the sumptuous red glow of the arch deepens right until the final moment.

A few miles farther and you reach the flaming rock fins known as Fiery Furnace, named for its golden late-afternoon glimmer. Beyond here an unpaved road leads 8 miles across Salt Valley to Klondike Bluffs, famed for the orange mono-liths known as "Marching Men".

The scenic drive ends at Devils Garden, home to the park's densest array of arches and fins. Several easy trails meander among its soaring spans. Sand Dune Arch shelters a large sand dune at its base; Skyline Arch became famous when a rockfall in 1940 doubled its size. A one-mile trail leads to Landscape Arch, a 306ft span of 'desert varnished' beige rock, thought to be the longest natural arch in the world. This slender span is so frail that hikers are not allowed up to or through the arch itself.

Delicate Arch

Rock pedestals

Double Arch

A Desert Cottontail

Bryce Canyon National Park

Snow storm in Bryce Canyon National Park

Roe deer

Hoodoos

Hummingbird

BRYCE CANYON

Encompassing the soft, limestone cliffs of southwestern Utah, Bryce Canyon National Park is a geologic fantasyland of rock towers, natural bridges, gravity-defying arches, precariously balanced rocks, and sky-filled windows carved deeply into the Paunsaugunt Plateau. Bryce Canyon is not actually a canyon – the park's primary features are a series of crescent-shaped natural amphitheatres and thin spires of rock known as hoodoos, throngs of red, yellow and orange pinnacles eating like the flames of a forest fire into the thickly wooded plateau. The name comes from the Mormon settler Ebenezer Bryce, who established a short-lived homestead nearby in 1874.

Bryce Amphitheater is the largest and most accessible, paralleled for its full length by the paved Rim Trail, which follows the lip of the plateau for just over 5 miles, between Sunrise and Sunset points. The best place to catch the dawn is actually Bryce Point, a mile or so further south at the southernmost tip of the amphitheatre.

Inspiration Point

The most popular trails in the park are those that drop into the amphitheatre itself. From Sunrise Point, the 1.8-mile round-trip Queen's Garden Trail descends the steep cliffs, joining up with the Navajo Loop Trail (1.3-mile round-trip), which drops down from Sunset Point and proceeds through the clustered formations of Silent City and the cool crevice known as Wall Street. In places, this awe-inspiring gulf of orange rock is less than 20ft wide, but it's too deep for the 800-year-old Douglas firs that grow from its sandy floor to poke their heads above the cliffs. The more strenuous, 5-mile Peekaboo Loop starts at Bryce Point and meanders through the amphitheatres' otherworldly formations.

Beyond Bryce Amphitheater, Hwy-63 – also known as the Scenic Drive – snakes for some 18-miles along the edge of the 8000ft plateau through forests of ponderosa pine and summer wildflowers. The 85ft-long Natural Bridge spans a steep gully approximately halfway along the route, before the road steadily climbs another thousand feet higher and continues south. Finally the ridge that it's following narrows to a slender neck, and the road is forced to end at the highest viewpoint of all, Rainbow Point (9105ft). Here, the ponderosa gives way to subalpine conifers, such as white fir and blue spruce. In the evenings, mule deer graze by the side of the road; in the daytime, rodents like ground squirrels and Utah prairie dogs, an endangered species, are often sighted.

Pine trees

Yellow flowers from a prickly pear cactus

Local fauna

Natural Bridge

Sky District, Canyonlands National Park

Eastern Fence Lizard

Candlestick Tower

Four O'Clock wildflower

CANYONLANDS

The largest and most magnificent of Utah's national parks, Canyonlands is a dizzying tangle of gorges, plateaus, fissures and faults, scattered with buttes and monoliths, pierced by arches and caverns, and penetrated only by a handful of dead-end roads. The park focuses upon the Y-shaped confluence of the Green and Colorado rivers, buried deep in the desert 40 miles southwest of Moab. With no way to get down to the rivers, the park splits naturally into three major sections.

The Needles district, east of the Colorado, is a red-rock wonderland of sandstone pinnacles and hidden meadows that's a favourite with hardy hikers and 4WD enthusiasts thanks to its intricate tracery of backcountry trails. While it has its share of long-range vistas, the Needles is noted primarily for its namesake thickets of candy-striped sandstone pillars. Clustered on scrubby rock outcrops, concealing pockets of incongruous grassland, these intriguing formations can be explored on brief forays or multi-day backpacking expeditions. The Squaw Flats Scenic Byway winds lazily into this section of the park, between cottonwood-lined Indian Creek and canyon walls of rich red sandstone.

Horseshoe Canyon

Pictograph rock art panel

Blooming Claret Cup cactus

Druid Arch

Pinyon Pine

This section also includes the park's only Confluence Overlook – a thousand feet below, the Green River flows in from the west, and the Colorado from the northeast. Sometimes the Green really is a pale green colour, and the Colorado almost red, tinted with dissolved red sandstone; at other times the Green is more of a yellow, and the Colorado a muddy chocolate.

The Maze district, west of both the Colorado and the Green, is a virtually inaccessible labyrinth of tortuous, waterless canyons. No roads entered the region until uranium prospectors arrived in the 1950s. Favoured destinations include Pictograph Canyon, ancient rock art that seems to record the moment when the Archaic people first acquired agriculture.

In the wedge of the "Y" between the two rivers, the high, dry mesa of the Island In The Sky district commands astonishing views across the whole park and beyond, seen from overlooks that can easily be toured by car. Grand View Point Overlook, at the southern end of the park road, commands a hundred-mile prospect of layer upon layer of naked sandstone, here stacked thousands of feet high, there fractured into bottomless canyons.

A fourth subsection of the park, Horseshoe Canyon in the west, was added to preserve the Southwest's finest collection of ancient rock art. Horseshoe Canyon Trail down to the Great Gallery ranks among the most beautiful hikes in Utah. Framed between the cottonwoods, a long row of dark, hollow-eyed, otherworldly entities stands stark against the pale rock. Archeologists believe the pictographs were produced by people of the Archaic culture, which flourished between 7500 BC and 500 AD.

CAPITOL REEF

One of the lesser-known parks in the Southwest, Capitol Reef National Park encompasses 75 miles of the Waterpocket Fold, a huge warp on the earth's surface that neatly bisects southeastern Utah. The Fold presented an almost impenetrable obstacle to nineteenth-century travellers, who therefore likened it to a reef on the ocean. Add the resemblance of the rounded "knobs" of white sandstone that top its central section to the US Capitol in Washington, and you have "Capitol Reef".

The one east–west highway, Hwy-24, crosses the park in under 20 miles, following the gorge of the Fremont River beneath tall sandstone cliffs – these open into a series of humpbacks, known to the Paiutes as 'the sleeping rainbow'.

The highway passes through the old village of Fruita, around the confluence of Sulphur Creek and the Fremont River. Abandoned in 1955, today the village comprises national park buildings, and a cluster of restored barns and houses among dense orchards – waxy, luxuriant green against the towering red cliffs, these hold almost three thousand trees planted by Mormon pioneers.

Other than Hwy-24, the only paved road in Capitol Reef is the Scenic Drive, which parallels the golden cliffs of the Waterpocket Fold for 8 miles south from the visitor centre. Successive individual pinnacles, such as Fern's Nipple and the Egyptian Temple, line the crest of the red-rock battlements to the east.

Capitol Reef's least accessible section is rugged Cathedral Valley, paralleling the northeastern exposure of the Fold. In among the heavily eroded red, blue and grey hills lie deep canyons and primeval gardens, populated by strange stone monoliths.

Barn in Fruita

ZION

Set in the rocky heart of southern Utah's canyon country, Zion National Park offers a dramatic juxtaposition of towering sandstone monoliths, narrow slot canyons, riverine forests, cascading waterfalls and myriad plant and wildlife. Desert flowers and cactuses provide unexpected flashes of colour in the uplands, as do darting hummingbirds. Isaac Behunin, who set up a log cabin here in 1862, dubbed the canyon "Little Zion" in the hope that it would serve as a place of refuge for Mormon pioneers. The canyon itself was protected in 1909 as Mukuntuweap National Monument; a larger area became Zion National Park in 1919.

The humble Virgin River (a tributary of the Colorado) carved Zion Canyon itself, the primary focus of the park today. A scenic drive parallels the tree-lined banks of the North Fork of the Virgin River and dead-ends beneath the natural rock amphitheatre known as the Temple of Sinawava. Along the way shady hiking trails branch off into the canyon, surrounded by dripping rocks and colourful hanging plants. Highlights on route include the Court of the Patriarchs, peaks named for Abraham, Isaac and Joseph arrayed around a small canyon west of the river, and the Emerald Pools Trail, a pink-paved path to delightfully cool seep-fed pools.

Zion Canyon

Court of the Patriarchs

Rock squirrel

Hiking trail towards the Zion Canyon Overlook

Narrows in Zion National Park

Temple of Sinawava

Bighorn sheep

Fall in Kolob Terrace

Zion Canyon view

The Scenic Drive ends at the start of the mile-long Riverside Walk. Walls of deep red sandstone soar to either side of the river, which is flanked by shimmering cottonwoods that turn a rich gold in the autumn. The Walk ends where the Virgin River emerges from the Narrows – upstream from here the river fills the entire gorge, a ravishing "slot canyon" often less than 20ft wide and channelled between vertical cliffs almost 1000ft high. The exhilarating Narrows day-hike involves wading upstream, against the current, 5 miles to Big Spring.

Kolob Terrace Road leads into the remoter central uplands of the park, while the Kolob Canyons section is easier to reach via I-15. Kolob Canyons Road twists alongside Taylor Creek and then up through Lee Pass, with countless trailheads and roadside viewpoints en route. Among Zion's very finest hikes, the 14-mile round-trip to Kolob Arch starts at Lee Pass, featuring superb close-up views of the finger canyons and the arch itself – one of world's longest natural rock spans at around 310ft. The road ends at a succession of narrow, red-walled "finger" canyons, each carved by a separate tiny stream; one, Hanging Valley, is interrupted by a sheer 1500ft cliff, stranding an isolated patch of thick forest far above the valley floor.

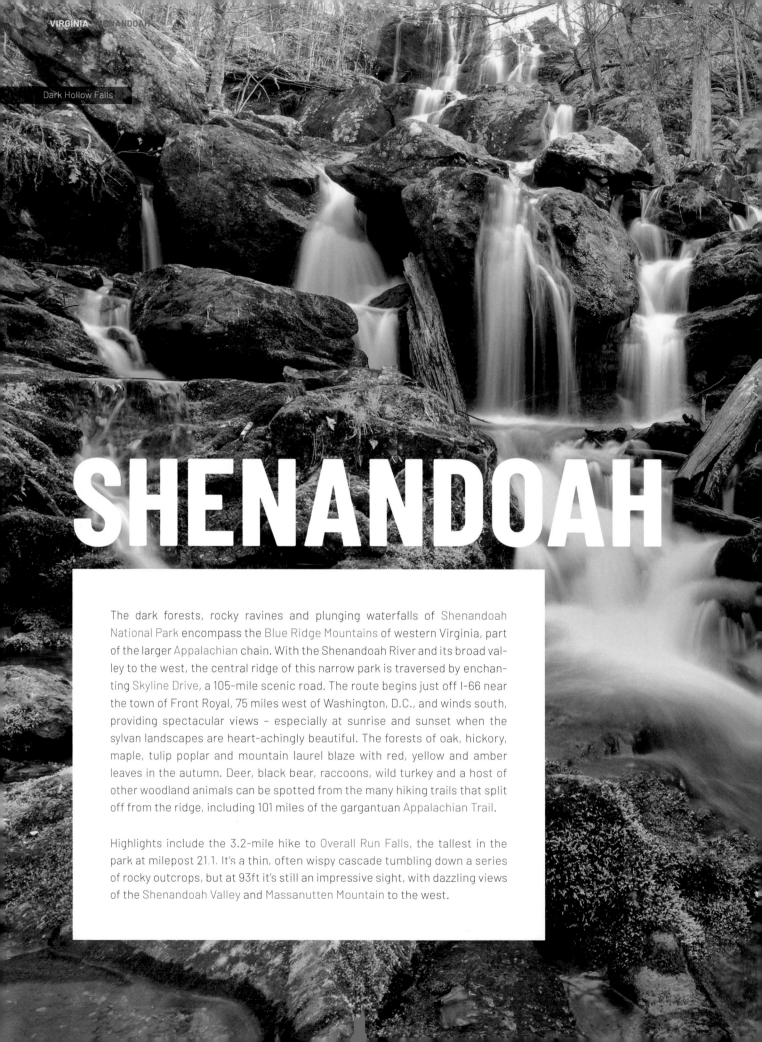

Dark Hollow Falls

SHENANDOAH

The dark forests, rocky ravines and plunging waterfalls of Shenandoah National Park encompass the Blue Ridge Mountains of western Virginia, part of the larger Appalachian chain. With the Shenandoah River and its broad valley to the west, the central ridge of this narrow park is traversed by enchanting Skyline Drive, a 105-mile scenic road. The route begins just off I-66 near the town of Front Royal, 75 miles west of Washington, D.C., and winds south, providing spectacular views – especially at sunrise and sunset when the sylvan landscapes are heart-achingly beautiful. The forests of oak, hickory, maple, tulip poplar and mountain laurel blaze with red, yellow and amber leaves in the autumn. Deer, black bear, raccoons, wild turkey and a host of other woodland animals can be spotted from the many hiking trails that split off from the ridge, including 101 miles of the gargantuan Appalachian Trail.

Highlights include the 3.2-mile hike to Overall Run Falls, the tallest in the park at milepost 21.1. It's a thin, often wispy cascade tumbling down a series of rocky outcrops, but at 93ft it's still an impressive sight, with dazzling views of the Shenandoah Valley and Massanutten Mountain to the west.

Whitetail Doe deer

Turk's cap lily flower

Colourful wildflower in Shenandoah National Park

Driving through Shenandoah National Park

Monarch and Painted Lady Butterflies

Sunrise above a foggy scene at the park

Family of black bears

Shenandoah National Park welcome sign

At mile marker 43, Old Rag Fire Road leads to the base of Old Rag Mountain (3284ft), where trails wriggle up a steep incline to the summit for panoramic views over the whole national park. Deer often scamper across the trail, with wildflowers carpeting the route in the spring. The path eventually emerges from the forest onto an exposed ridge, littered with giant granite boulders – making it to the top involves climbing, crawling and clambering over and around them.

Big Meadows lies in the heart of the park, home to the Byrd Visitor Center and a huge grassland area previously used as farmland. Today it's kept clear through controlled fires and mowing, allowing for carpets of wildflowers in

the spring, as well as butterflies, white-tailed deer and a plethora of birdlife. Outside the Visitor Center, a shirtless statue of "Iron Mike" commemorates Civilian Conservation Corps workers who built much of the park infrastructure in the 1930s. A short trail runs to picturesque Dark Hollow Falls, which cascades 70ft over a series of ledges amidst dense woodland. Just to the south, Milam Gap marks the start of a 2-mile hike to Rapidan Camp, where President Hoover established a trout-fishing retreat on the Rapidan River in 1929. The main cabin, the Brown House, has been restored to its original appearance.

View of Shenandoah Valley from Skyline Drive

Downtown Seattle with Mount Rainier in the background

Marmot

Red Fox

Narada Falls

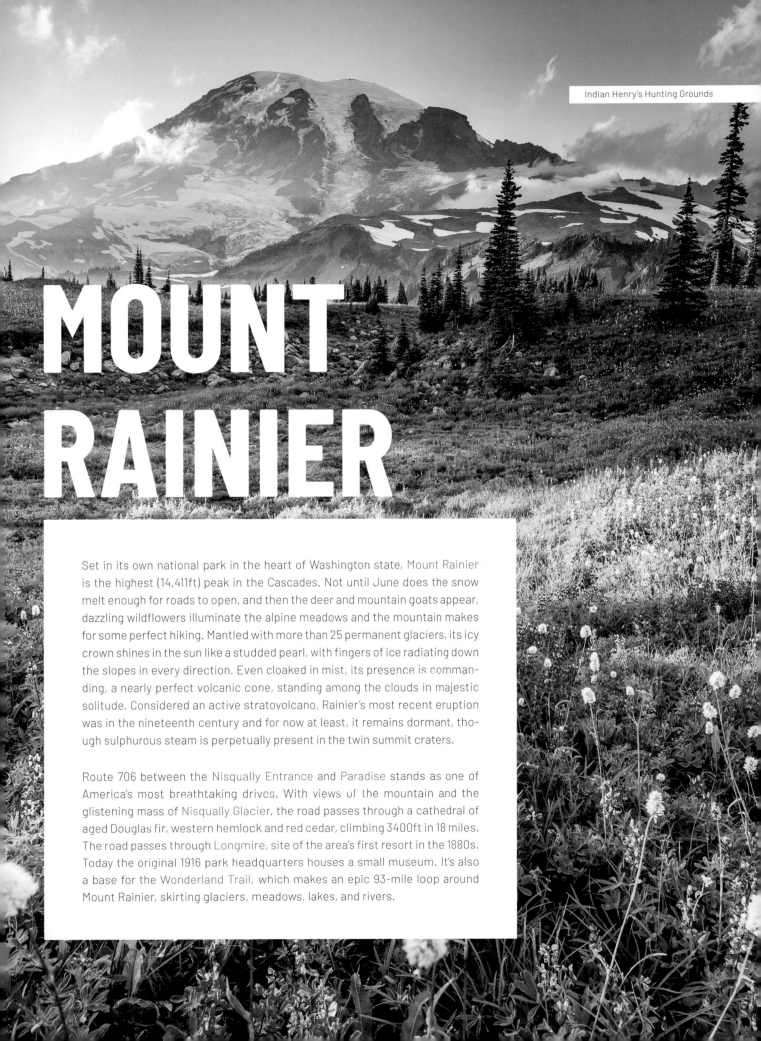

MOUNT RAINIER

Set in its own national park in the heart of Washington state, Mount Rainier is the highest (14,411ft) peak in the Cascades. Not until June does the snow melt enough for roads to open, and then the deer and mountain goats appear, dazzling wildflowers illuminate the alpine meadows and the mountain makes for some perfect hiking. Mantled with more than 25 permanent glaciers, its icy crown shines in the sun like a studded pearl, with fingers of ice radiating down the slopes in every direction. Even cloaked in mist, its presence is commanding, a nearly perfect volcanic cone, standing among the clouds in majestic solitude. Considered an active stratovolcano, Rainier's most recent eruption was in the nineteenth century and for now at least, it remains dormant, though sulphurous steam is perpetually present in the twin summit craters.

Route 706 between the Nisqually Entrance and Paradise stands as one of America's most breathtaking drives. With views of the mountain and the glistening mass of Nisqually Glacier, the road passes through a cathedral of aged Douglas fir, western hemlock and red cedar, climbing 3400ft in 18 miles. The road passes through Longmire, site of the area's first resort in the 1880s. Today the original 1916 park headquarters houses a small museum. It's also a base for the Wonderland Trail, which makes an epic 93-mile loop around Mount Rainier, skirting glaciers, meadows, lakes, and rivers.

Mount Rainier

From Longmire, the road continues along the Nisqually River, winding and switchbacking past Narada Falls, a stunning 168ft plunge of water right next to the road, and on to the main visitor centre at Paradise. Home of historic Paradise Inn, a rustic gem built of local cedar in 1916, this is also a major trail hub. The 1.2-mile Nisqually Vista Trail loops past glorious splashes of Indian paintbrush, shooting star, and dozens of other wildflowers that follow the retreating melt line up the slope in the summer. For a tougher hike, the Skyline Trail makes a 5-mile loop to the 6,800ft Panorama Point, with sensational views of Nisqually Glacier and the Cascade Range. The 5-mile Lakes Trail leads to Reflection Lakes and Louise Lake, both placid tarns that reflect Rainier as well as any mirror.

Paradise is also a staging area for most attempts on Mount Rainier's summit, though the 18-mile, two-day trek is extremely strenuous and should only be undertaken by experienced climbers.

Climbing Mout Rainier

Colourful bursts of wildflower

Indian Paintbrush

Nisqually Glacier

NORTH CASCADES

Set deep in the Cascade Mountains of northern Washington state, this national park comprises two main sections bisected by the Skagit River. It's primarily untouched wilderness, with high jagged peaks, deep valleys, shimmering lakes, more than 300 glaciers, and countless waterfalls. Hwy-20 (also known as the North Cascades Highway) cuts between the two sections, following the Skagit Gorge within the Ross Lake National Recreation Area. The main visitor centre stands in the small village of Newhalem, created by Seattle City Light in the 1920s to house workers who built the three dams that lie farther upstream – the Gorge, Diablo and Ross. Back on the highway there are stunning views of Gorge Creek Falls, one of hundreds of cataracts that tumble down the mountains, while from Diablo, a strenuous 10-mile round trip on Sourdough Mountain Trail leads to a gorgeous panorama of lakes, glaciers and surrounding peaks. The Diablo Lake Overlook presents a mesmerizing panorama of snow-capped ranges, with the glacier-carved pinnacles of Colonial Peak and Ruby Mountain, both over 7000ft, rising to the south.

The southern area of the park is even more remote, with the only road access via the bumpy, gravelly Cascade River Road, which makes a winding 30-mile climb from Marblemount's Wilderness Information Center toward Cascade Pass. From here a trail follows the Stehekin River to Lake Chelan's isolated but busy north shore in the Lake Chelan National Recreation Area.

Diablo Lake Overlook

OLYMPIC

Magnificent Olympic National Park, comprising the colossal mountains in the heart of the Olympic Peninsula plus a separate, isolated 60-mile strip of Pacific coastline farther west, is one of Washington's prime wilderness destinations. It features torrid rivers, alpine meadows of wildflowers in summer, sizeable tracts of moss-draped rainforest and boundless opportunities for spectacular hiking and wildlife watching. There are no roads that go through the middle of the park, but instead enter the interior from its edge like spokes on a wheel.

The main visitor centre stands in Port Angeles, where a 17-mile scenic road winds its way up to Hurricane Ridge. At 5242ft, this affords mesmerizing views of the jagged peaks around Mount Olympus itself, clothed in the pearly-white robe of Blue Glacier and at 7980ft, the park's highest point (the peak is only accessible to professional mountaineers). Seven glaciers hang from Olympus; its massive shoulders have been draped in ice for thousands of years, though its glaciers continue to decrease in size.

Hoh Rain Forest

Lake Crescent, Olympic National Park

Sol Duc Falls

Bainbridge Island Ferry Dock

Ruby Beach

Barred owl

Mount Olympus and the Blue Glacier

Hurricane Ridge

Mountain Goat

Heading west from Port Angeles, US-101 skirts picturesque Lake Crescent, a misty tarn hemmed in by densely wooded mountains. A short walk on the Marymere Falls Trail leads to a lovely 90ft cascade, just one of dozens that gush over mountain ridges throughout the park. Further along US-101 another road branches south up the Sol Duc River valley, where hiking trails run up to the moss-covered rocks and gentle cascades of Sol Duc Falls and its popular hot springs – three outdoor pools (and one unheated swimming pool) with mineral-rich waters bubbling up at 99 to 104°F.

Veiled in mist, a scattering of rock arches, "sea stacks" and tiny islands gives the wilder Pacific coast section of the park a dreamy quality. Harbour seals haul out on the rocks; bald eagles prowl the skies; otters float on their backs in kelp beds, using stones to crack shellfish; raccoons, skunks and an occasional black bear wander toward the water looking for a meal. Black rocks jut out of the sea at Rialto Beach, while inviting Ruby Beach is named for its red-and-black-pebbled sand.

The far western portion of the park contains the Hoh Rain Forest, one of the world's largest temperate rainforests. The perpetual mist and showers here, together with a deep layer of decaying organic matter, produce subalpine fir and other trees – mostly Sitka spruce and western hemlock – of truly gargantuan size. From the visitor centre the Hall of Mosses Trail cuts through a leafy canopy of big leaf maple, spruce and red cedar draped with large growths of spikemoss. The endangered spotted owl makes its home here, and black bear, black-tailed deer and Roosevelt elk are occasionally seen feeding in the underbrush.

NEW RIVER GORGE

Despite its name, the New River is one of the oldest rivers on the continent, taking millions of years to cut through the gorge. Spanning 70,000 acres, the New River Gorge National Park and Preserve was added to the US national park system in December 2020, with food, lodging and guided activities also available. Nestled between Beckley and Hico on Hwy-19, New River Gorge is located in southern West Virginia.

Despite its impressive geology, the region was heavily shaped by its coal industry in the eighteenth and nineteenth centuries. There are old stone walls, original house foundations and coal mine entrances still visible on multiple hikes. Take the African American Heritage tour to hear the stories of the various coal miners and railroad workers who worked here and learn more about Carter G. Woodson, founder of the Association for the Study of African American Life and History, who spent many years working as a coal miner here.

Industry work aside, the flora and fauna of this park are in abundance. The V-shaped gorge is carpeted by Appalachian vegetation and thick layers of sedimentary rock expose its 300-million-year-old history. There are 65 species of mammals in the park – white-tailed deer, elusive black bear, red and grey foxes – along with around 40 species of reptiles, amphibians, fish and plenty of other visible wildlife.

Among the numerous hiking routes, the 5.6-mile Glade Creek trail is ideal for moderate fitness levels and features a number of cascades and waterfalls, making it an ideal spot for a quick dip!

The gorge from Grandview Overlook

Moulton Barn, with the Grand Teton behind

GRAND TETON

The jagged tooth-like peaks of Grand Teton National Park are a magnificent spectacle, sheer-faced cliffs rising abruptly some 7000ft above the valley floor. A string of gem-like lakes is set tight at the foot of the mountains; the park also encompasses the broad, sagebrush-covered Jackson Hole river basin (a "hole" was a pioneer term for a flat, mountain-ringed valley), broken by the gently winding Snake River, home to elk, bison and moose.

At the heart of the park lies tranquil Jackson Lake, a glacial remnant rich in trout and mountain whitefish. From Colter Bay Visitor Center rented boats, canoes and kayaks cruise the calm, icy fresh waters, ringed by dense forests of spruce and fir. Elegant Jackson Lake Lodge sits right on the water offering mesmerizing views, while Signal Mountain offers a breathtaking panorama of the lake and the Tetons beyond.

Bighorn ram

Maud Noble Cabin

Mountain valley in Grand Teton

Hidden Falls

Grazing buffalo

American Bald Eagles

Schwabacher Landing, Grand Teton National Park

Teton Thistle

Crystal-clear Jenny Lake is another hub for boating, kayaking and scenic hiking trails. Ferries shuttle across the lake for a face-to-face encounter with towering, partly hunchbacked Grand Teton (Wyoming's second highest mountain) at Inspiration Point. Wildflowers poke through the rocks, and marmots scurry across the trails while clouds shroud the snow-capped summits. The moderate Jenny Lake Trail loops around the lake, the mountains reflected perfectly in its pristine waters. The trail passes through glades of spruce and thimbleberries, with detours to gurgling Hidden Falls and the Moose Ponds, where moose really do come to drink.

Moose village, on the Snake River south of Jenny Lake, is home to the beautifully designed Craig Thomas Discovery & Visitor Center. The park's geology, ecology and human history are brought to life through illuminating exhibits, artwork and movies. From here it's possible to float (on giant inner tubes), canoe or kayak down the Snake River, or explore nearby Menors Ferry Historic District. Pioneer and ferryman Bill Menor arrived in 1894, and his rustic homestead cabin and store has been artfully preserved, along with a replica of his cable ferry. Exhibits inside the timbered Maud Noble Cabin shed light on the portentous meeting that took place here in 1923 to discuss the formation of the park. Set on a wind-blown plain, Mormon Row is where Mormon homesteaders settled in the 1890s, and several timber barns and homes remain standing. The Moulton Barn is positioned especially photogenically, with the snow-capped Tetons framed perfectly in the background.

Canoeing on Jackson Lake

Howling wolf in Yellowstone

Mammoth Hot Springs

Herd of heavy-bearded bison

Norris Geyser Basin

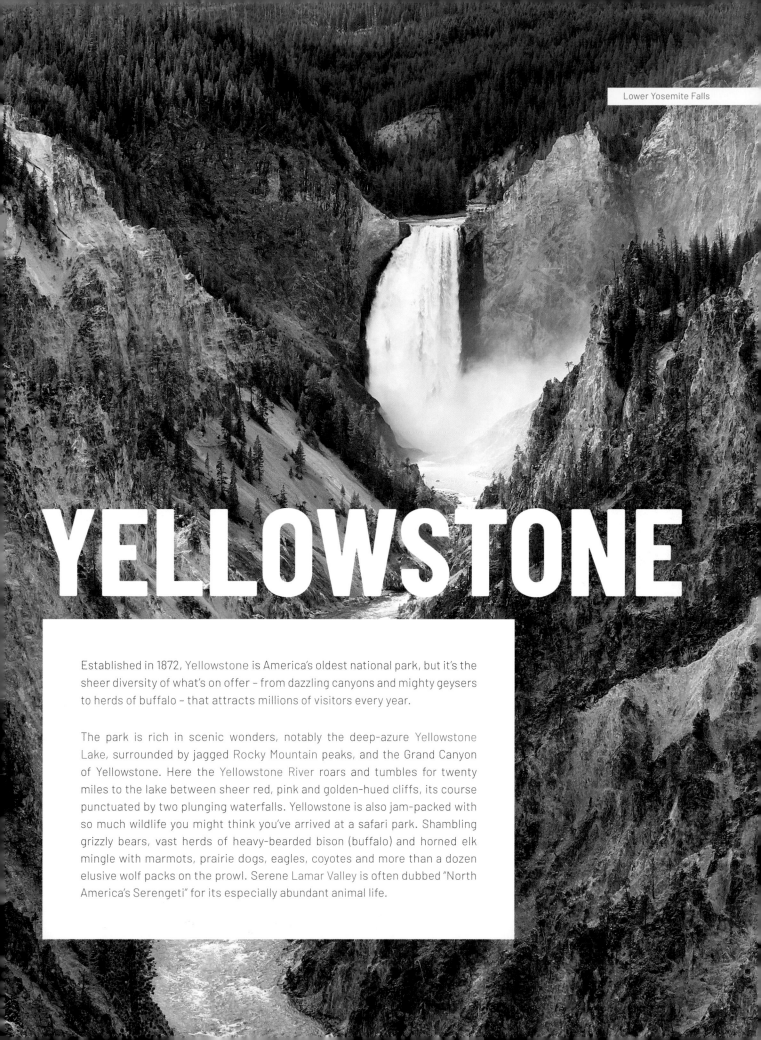

Lower Yosemite Falls

YELLOWSTONE

Established in 1872, Yellowstone is America's oldest national park, but it's the sheer diversity of what's on offer – from dazzling canyons and mighty geysers to herds of buffalo – that attracts millions of visitors every year.

The park is rich in scenic wonders, notably the deep-azure Yellowstone Lake, surrounded by jagged Rocky Mountain peaks, and the Grand Canyon of Yellowstone. Here the Yellowstone River roars and tumbles for twenty miles to the lake between sheer red, pink and golden-hued cliffs, its course punctuated by two plunging waterfalls. Yellowstone is also jam-packed with so much wildlife you might think you've arrived at a safari park. Shambling grizzly bears, vast herds of heavy-bearded bison (buffalo) and horned elk mingle with marmots, prairie dogs, eagles, coyotes and more than a dozen elusive wolf packs on the prowl. Serene Lamar Valley is often dubbed "North America's Serengeti" for its especially abundant animal life.

What really sets Yellowstone apart, however, is that this is one of the world's largest volcanoes, with thermal activity providing half the world's geysers, thousands of fumaroles jetting plumes of steam, mud pots gurgling with acid-dissolved muds and clays, and, of course, hot springs. The park might not look like a volcano, but that's because the caldera is so big – 34 by 45 miles – and because, thankfully, it hasn't exploded for 640,000 years. Of the geysers, Old Faithful erupts more frequently than any other – the first sign of activity is a soft hissing as water splashes repeatedly over its mud-caked rim, and after several minutes, a column of water shoots to a height of 180ft. The nearby Grand Geyser blows its top on average just twice daily, for twelve to twenty minutes, in a series of four powerful bursts that can reach 200ft. Other highlights include the fluorescent intensity of the Grand Prismatic Spring at Midway Geyser Basin, and the Norris Geyser Basin, a pallid landscape of whistling vents and fumaroles. At Mammoth Hot Springs terraces of barnacle-like deposits cascade down a vapour-shrouded mountainside, tinted a marvellous array of greys, greens, yellows, browns and oranges.

The park is open year-round. Blanketed in snow between November and April, Yellowstone takes on a magical appearance in winter, when snowcoaches, skis and snowmobiles replace cars. Waterfalls freeze in mid-plunge, geysers blast towering plumes of steam and water into the crisp air and bison graze stoically, beards matted with ice.

Grand Prismatic Spring

The National Park of American Samoa

AMERICAN SAMOA

Located 2600 miles south-southwest of Hawaii, American Samoa is a United States territory of five volcanic islands and two coral atolls. The National Park of American Samoa, established in 1988, encompasses nearly 9000 acres on three separate islands, a tropical paradise of blissfully untouched rainforest, coral beaches and jungle-smothered peaks. The park also contains a remarkable variety of wildlife, including dozens of tropical birds and fish, tortoises, the Pacific boa, and the rare flying fox (actually a large bat).

Rainforest dominates the Tutuila Island section of the park, set just to the north of the capital Pago Pago. Trails fan out across the park and up to the top of Mount 'Alava, where steep ladders end at an abandoned tramway once used to transport visitors to the summit – an awe-inspiring panorama of Pago Pago Harbour spreads out below.

The park on remote Ta'u Island is also mostly undisturbed rainforest, containing the sacred site of Saua, considered by many to be the birthplace of the Polynesian people. Beautiful sea cliffs drop from the top of Lata Mountain, the highest peak in the territory. At 3000ft, these cliffs are the tallest in the world. Tiny Ofu Island contains a beach of fine coral sand and coconut palms, considered to be the loveliest in Samoa, and also one of the most exceptional coral reefs in the Pacific.

Pago Pago Harbour

White-collared Flying Fox (Fruit Bat)

Ofu Island

Cruz Bay, St John

Coral reef, St Croix

Orchid tree, St John

Anchored yachts, St John

Green Turtle at the Frederiksted Pier, St Croix

VIRGIN ISLANDS

Occupying two thirds of St. John, one of the US Virgin Islands, Virgin Islands National Park boasts ravishing Caribbean beaches and coral reefs rich in marine life. The laid-back town of Cruz Bay is the gateway to the park, connected to the outside world by boat. Pristine Trunk Bay, long Cinnamon Bay and tranquil Honeymoon beaches are some of the world's most beautiful, featuring soft chalk-white sands under tall palm trees. Crystal-clear Trunk Bay features an underwater snorkelling trail laced with candy-coloured fish. The seagrass in Maho Bay attracts sea turtles and stingrays, while protected Salt Pond Bay is also ideal for snorkelling. Fragile elkhorn coral reefs lie just off idyllic Hawksnest Beach, a playground for juvenile tropical fish, squid and turtles.

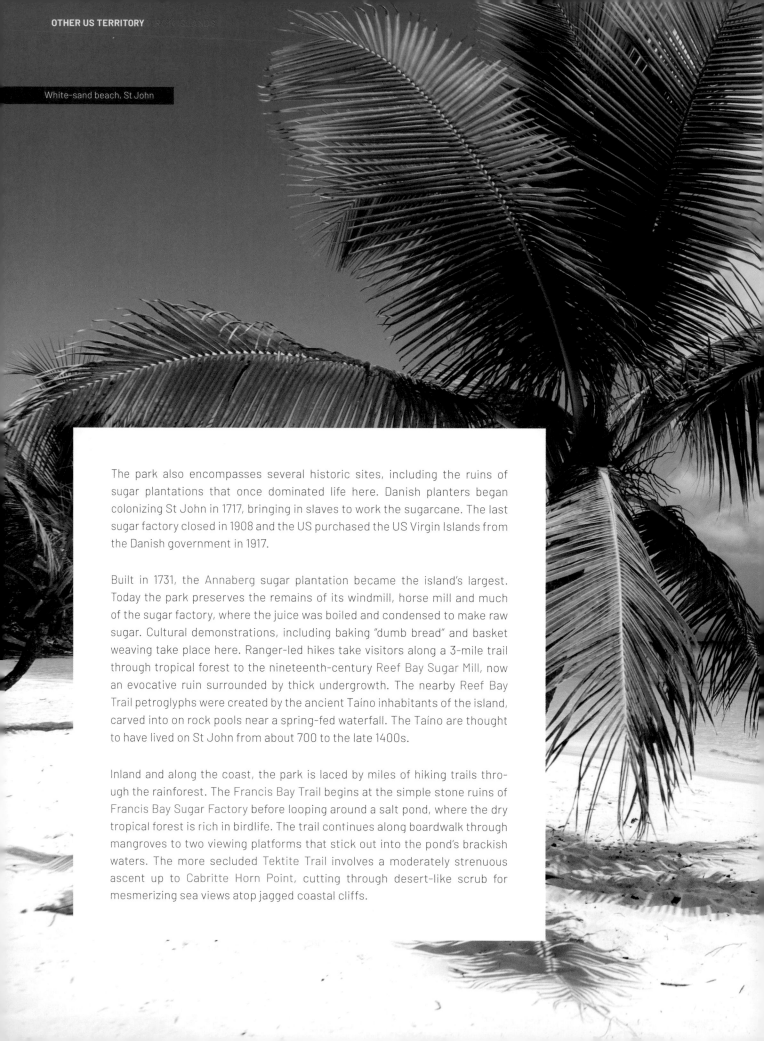

White-sand beach, St John

The park also encompasses several historic sites, including the ruins of sugar plantations that once dominated life here. Danish planters began colonizing St John in 1717, bringing in slaves to work the sugarcane. The last sugar factory closed in 1908 and the US purchased the US Virgin Islands from the Danish government in 1917.

Built in 1731, the Annaberg sugar plantation became the island's largest. Today the park preserves the remains of its windmill, horse mill and much of the sugar factory, where the juice was boiled and condensed to make raw sugar. Cultural demonstrations, including baking "dumb bread" and basket weaving take place here. Ranger-led hikes take visitors along a 3-mile trail through tropical forest to the nineteenth-century Reef Bay Sugar Mill, now an evocative ruin surrounded by thick undergrowth. The nearby Reef Bay Trail petroglyphs were created by the ancient Taíno inhabitants of the island, carved into on rock pools near a spring-fed waterfall. The Taíno are thought to have lived on St John from about 700 to the late 1400s.

Inland and along the coast, the park is laced by miles of hiking trails through the rainforest. The Francis Bay Trail begins at the simple stone ruins of Francis Bay Sugar Factory before looping around a salt pond, where the dry tropical forest is rich in birdlife. The trail continues along boardwalk through mangroves to two viewing platforms that stick out into the pond's brackish waters. The more secluded Tektite Trail involves a moderately strenuous ascent up to Cabritte Horn Point, cutting through desert-like scrub for mesmerizing sea views atop jagged coastal cliffs.

Windmill ruin, Annaberg

Ancient Taino petroglyphs, St John

Hawksnest Bay Beach, Virgin Islands National Park

Clock Tower, St Croix

INDEX

AUTHOR

Stephen Keeling has been exploring America's national parks since 1991. He worked as a financial journalist for seven years before writing his first travel guide and has since written numerous titles for Rough Guides. Stephen lives in New York City.

PHOTO CREDITS